ON EARTH AS IT IS IN HEAVEN

ROBERT GRIFFITH

Copyright © 2024 Grace and Truth Publishing

All rights reserved. No part of this book may be reproduced, stored in a retrieval system, or transmitted in any form, without the written permission of Grace and Truth Publishing.

GRACE AND TRUTH PUBLISHING
PO Box 338, Gunnedah NSW 2380 Australia
www.graceandtruthpublishing.com.au

All Bible quotes are from the New International Version (NIV) expect where otherwise stated.

NEW INTERNATIONAL VERSION (NIV), Copyright 1973, 1978 and 1984 by international Bible Society. Used by permission of Zondervan Publishing House. All rights reserved.

Other version quotes are from:

AMPLIFIED BIBLE (AMP), Copyright © 1954, 1958, 1962, 1964, 1965, 1987 by The Lockman Foundation. Used by permission.

ENGLISH STANDARD VERSION (ESV), Copyright © 2001 by Crossway Bibles, a division of Good News Publishers. Used by permission. All rights reserved.

NEW AMERICAN STANDARD BIBLE (NASB), Copyright © 1960, 1962, 1963, 1968, 1971, 1972, 1973, 1975, 1977, by The Lockman Foundation. Used by permission.

NEW KING JAMES VERSION (NKJV), Copyright © 1979, 1980, 1982, by Thomas Nelson Inc. Used by permission. All rights reserved.

THE MESSAGE (MSG), by Eugene Peterson, Copyright © 1993, 1994, 1995, 1996, and 2000. Used by permission of NavPress Publishing Group. All rights reserved.

REVISED STANDARD VERSION (RSV), Copyright © 1973, by Thomas Nelson Inc. Used by permission. All rights reserved.

Quotes in square brackets are the author's comment.

ISBN 978-0-6486439-5-1

TABLE OF CONTENTS

1 Embracing our Purpose 5

2 Heaven Has Come to Earth 18

3 The Gate is Open 29

4 In His Presence 40

5 Why Did Jesus Come? 52

6 Living in the Kingdom of Heaven 63

7 Wisdom and Power 72

8 Embracing a Kingdom Worldview 83

9 The Mystery of the Kingdom 93

10 The Hard Truth 104

11 The Presence of the Future 115

12 The Core Value of the Kingdom 125

13 Hidden Treasure 130

PREFACE

I think I could safely say that what we call *The Lord's Prayer* is undoubtedly the most prayed prayer of all time. Many millions of people have prayed this prayer hundreds of thousands of times during their life. Towards the beginning of this model prayer the Lord Jesus gave His disciples, we have these amazing words, *"Your Kingdom come, Your will be done, on earth as it is in heaven."* These words are prayed tens of thousands of times every hour across the world. They are so easy to pray, but do we know what we are asking? Do we have the slightest idea what our life, our church, the whole world would be like if that prayer was answered?

Many people see the Kingdom of heaven as a future reality. Heaven is what follows this life when we die. Whilst that is true, the idea that heaven is also a present reality, here and now, in my life, my church and in this dysfunctional, broken world, is something many people never really grasp.

The thought that we should all be embracing the reality and the power of the Kingdom of heaven here and now in our lives, is almost blasphemous to some believers. I am not sure what they think it means for God's Kingdom to come and God's will to be done on earth, as it is in heaven. The words are not ambiguous.

Jesus clearly asked us to pray, and believe, that what is real in heaven, would progressively become real on earth. He then gave us all that we need to live as those who are committed to bringing the reality of the heaven to earth.

That incredible, mind-blowing concept is the subject of this book and I invite you now to strap yourself in as we take this journey together.

- Robert Griffith

CHAPTER ONE
Embracing our Purpose

Throughout the course of my life and ministry, I have often taken a few moments to pause and ask myself the crucial question: *Why am I here?* Sometimes I ask this question when I'm in a state of peaceful reflection, looking perhaps for clarification regarding my purpose in life. This is done to ensure that I do not waste any time pursuing causes that are not God's causes and to be sure I'm not following dreams which God has not given me.

Then there are those other times when I am absolutely exhausted from the fight and I am just attempting to navigate the turbulent waters we so often encounter in front-line ministry. I could be battling hostility, apathy, treachery, or spiritual attacks. It is at those points in my journey when the question becomes a little more desperate, "*Why am I here?!*"

In all instances, the response is always the same, presuming that I am listening to God and not my tormented mind or the devil. In reality, the meaning of my life is crystal clear, and I realise that I already know the answer to that question before I ask it. It's possible that all I need at such times is God's fresh affirmation and encouragement.

The driving force in my thinking and the over-arching reason I do what I do, happens to be what also defines the purpose of the church on earth.

So, I want to suggest from the start of this book that, in the final analysis, we are all here for the same reason, and that reason is embodied in that one line in the prayer which Jesus instructed His disciples to pray a very long time ago. You might even say that this is where our defining purpose originates.

This prayer is referred to as *The Lord's Prayer*. However, that name is quite misleading because it is a prayer that includes a confession of sin, and Jesus did not have any sin throughout His life. Therefore, this was not the personal prayer of the Lord; rather, it is a pattern prayer or an example prayer that the Lord gave to His followers, and via the Spirit and the Bible, to us also.

This is the reason why an increasing number of biblical scholars and preachers refer to this prayer now as *The Disciples Prayer* or, as I saw in one Bible translation recently, *The Model Prayer*.

Since the day when Jesus gave this model prayer to His disciples, hundreds of millions of His followers have now committed this prayer to memory and prayed it both privately and collectively many times – some even daily.

Now I don't have a problem with that; but there is always a risk that memorised prayers and Scriptures can lose their power and their profound meaning if they are recited in a ritualistic manner, and this prayer has most certainly been used in this way by many millions of believers.

Personally, I find it really challenging to say that whole prayer without pausing at each individual phrase to contemplate the significance of the words and the implications they carry. I could deliver an entire sermon on practically every phrase, and many preachers have done exactly that. It has a great deal of depth and significance. I want to focus on the first portion of this prayer as we begin this study together.

"*Our Father*" is the first place to pause and notice that it does not say "*My Father*." As I am sure you know, in our western culture, the focus is frequently placed on the individual. This probably why the majority of people reciting The Lord's prayer, miss the importance of the very first word.

There has never been a time in our culture when the emphasis on our individual rights has been higher than it is now. The majority of advertising is purposefully centred on the wants and perceived need of individuals.

It's not a coincidence therefore that Jesus tells us right at the beginning, before we start praying for anything else, that we are a family, a community. We are not just individuals.

Beginning with "*Our Father*" and concluding with "*Yours is the Kingdom,*" this prayer essentially conveys the idea that God's Kingdom is synonymous with the concept of family.

In other words, if we take ourselves out of the context of family, of community, we effectively remove ourselves from the power and reality of the Kingdom of heaven.

The term Kingdom refers to the domain that is technically under the control of the King. The domain that is under the dominion of the King is known as the Kingdom, and the King of the Kingdom of heaven is the Lord Jesus Christ.

Therefore, when we witness the dominion of this King come upon a person who has torment, they obtain peace of mind. If we witness the dominion of this King coming upon someone who is afflicted with cancer, we see that person free of the disease.

As a result, when the Bible instructs us to "*Seek first His Kingdom,*" how that happens is contingent upon the nature of the problem that we are attempting to solve at the time.

For example, if you're ministering to someone in poverty then the Kingdom of heaven will shatter the spirit of poverty and put that person into a position of increase and blessing. Why is that? It's simply because in this Kingdom, there is no poverty. To seek first His Kingdom is not a generic prayer to God in which we proclaim, *"Someday, I want to go to heaven."*

It is a specific petition which says, *"I'm looking for Your dominion to be realized; to be manifested; to be revealed in this situation here and now."*

In Matthew 12:28 Jesus said, *"If I cast a demon out of you by the Spirit of God, then the kingdom of God has come upon you."* So, what is Jesus doing here? He's talking to an individual who is tortured by devils and he effectively says, *"If I get that demon out of you, it's only because the Kingdom of heaven collided with the Kingdom of darkness and the Kingdom of heaven always wins."*

That means all of us are ministers of the Kingdom of heaven or the Kingdom of God - the two names mean the same thing and are used interchangeably throughout the Bible.

As citizens of God's Kingdom, we don't just carry a message, we actually carry a message that represents a presence – the presence of the King. We truly release something and Someone - we are distributors of His reign and stewards of His presence.

To seek first the Kingdom of heaven means that in any given situation, we are looking for God's solution for that problem and God's presence and ability to bring that answer to effect.

This means at the very outset; we have to carry a hope and a firm confidence that God has an answer now for any and every difficulty we face, no matter how small or great. Sometimes we see the benefits and the breakthrough instantly, at other times it takes patience and hard work as we wait upon the Lord.

Those times can be painful but they're also a crucial part of our faith journey. Ok let's get to the line from which this whole book emerges and in which I feel the whole Church must find its true purpose.

> *"Our Father who art in heaven, hallowed be your name, your kingdom come, your will be done on earth as it is in heaven." (Matthew 6:9-10)*

Now this is where some knowledge of New Testament Greek is very beneficial. In the original language for this specific verse, it doesn't read as a prayer calling for the Kingdom to arrive. In the Greek it actually reads more like an edict. So, it could be translated, *"Kingdom of God, come! Will of God, be done!"* It's a bold declaration and so Jesus is telling His disciples, then and now, to declare that heaven has come and will come to earth. Or to put it another way, what is true in heaven in eternity will increasingly become true on earth here and now!

I recall when the true meaning of this sentence first unfolded for me many years ago. I felt a burning conviction inside me and I found that I could no longer accept things that exist in this world that don't exist in the Kingdom of heaven. Things like sickness, sin, disease, deception, death, discouragement, doubt, fear, evil, pride, loneliness, isolation, racism, hatred, envy … etc.

None of these things exist in the Kingdom of heaven, so as that Kingdom eclipses the kingdom of this world, we should loathe those things more than ever and our desire to unleash the full power and reality of heaven into the dysfunction and darkness of this world should continue to rise up within us daily.

It has also been said that there will be no shadows in heaven. I'll bet you haven't thought much about that, have you?

Let me share a few Scriptures here:

> *"Every good gift and every perfect gift is from above, and comes down from the Father of lights, with whom there is no variation or shadow of turning." (James 1:17)*

"God is light and in Him is no darkness at all." (1 John 1:5)

"The city had no need of the sun or of the moon to shine in it, for the glory of God illuminated it. The Lamb is its light." (Revelation 21:23)

What generates shadows in this world? The sun, the moon and many different man-made light sources. Well, none of those exist in the Kingdom of heaven. In the Kingdom of heaven, <u>God</u> is the only source of light and He is beaming everywhere all at once. We have shadows here on earth because we have light coming in one direction from somewhere to somewhere else and anything in between casts a shadow.

In the Kingdom of heaven, the light source is only God, Who is everywhere simultaneously. He doesn't come from somewhere or go to somewhere - He just is - all the time. That's why there are no shadows in heaven. What does that teach us? It teaches us that in heaven, everything is directly tied to the presence and to the identity of God Himself.

Therefore, if we are going to pray that the reality of God's world will manifest in this world, it's crucial that we appreciate what heaven values. By far the highest value in heaven is the presence of God. So, when we pray or declare, *'Your Kingdom Come'* we are releasing the presence of God into this earthly kingdom and into every scenario over which we make that declaration.

It is my prayer that as we progress through this book, we will be asking ourselves what does it look like to establish a culture in our lives, in our families and in our churches, that is rooted in, revolves around and finds its identity and purpose within the presence of God? If that is the highest value in the Kingdom of heaven, then it goes without saying that this should always be the highest priority of the church, but sadly that is not the case.

For most of my life and ministry, so many people in the church which bears the name of Jesus Christ, have been clearly oriented towards numerical increase.

In fact, we even have a name for this approach - it's called the *'Church growth'* movement and in the last fifty years there have been thousands of books produced; hundreds of thousands of conferences run; and many millions of sermons preached, which are all centred on one thing: growing the church.

I believe if only a fraction of the energy, time, money, resources and emotion we have invested in the Church Growth movement was effective, the Body of Christ on earth would be 1,000 times greater than it is now. So why isn't it? It's certainly not for a lack of commitment, enthusiasm, effort and prayer!

The reason the Church Growth movement has failed is because it was defective from its inception. That is because, quite simply, it was not our responsibility to grow the church in the first place!

In Matthew 16:18 we read where Jesus made a promise to us all, *"I will build my Church and the gates of hell will not prevail against it."* It is crucial that we acknowledge the authority of Christ's Word here.

World missions are not dependent on human initiative, human wisdom or human perseverance. The success of world missions is ultimately dependent on the strength, the faithfulness, and the wisdom of the risen, living Christ to keep His promise to us all: *"I will build my Church."*

Jesus didn't say, *"You will build My Church."* Jesus also didn't say, *"Missionaries will build My Church."* Jesus didn't even say, *"Pastors will build My Church."* Jesus clearly said, *"I will build My Church."*

The Apostle Paul realised this and he was jealous to always offer praise to Jesus. In Romans 15:18, Paul declares, "*I will not presume to speak of anything except what Christ has accomplished through me.*" Christ accomplished it. Jesus Christ brought about the obedience of the people. Yes, missionaries are vital. Pastors and elders are important. But we are not ultimate. Only the presence of God in Christ is ultimate and only Jesus Christ ever has the right to say, "*I will build My Church.*"

Church growth has always been the responsibility of the Lord of the church, Jesus Christ and He promised to build His church. Church planting and establishment is a supernatural work and without that supernatural work, all we really have is a human organization which lacks the power to achieve anything in the Kingdom of heaven. This was the clear point in how Matthew ended his gospel, reporting where Jesus said:

> "*All authority has been given to Me in heaven and on earth. Go therefore and make disciples of all the countries.*"
> *(Matthew 28:18-19)*

Jesus effectively says here, "*I have authority to do it – authority over all the powers of darkness, over death and hell, over governments and terrorists – and I will do it. I will build My Church. So now go and make disciples.*" Making disciples of Christ is our responsibility, our calling and our commission from Jesus. We are called to lead people to a person, Jesus, Who is the One Who will transform their hearts. Then we help them grow in their new relationship.

We were never called to enrol people in an institution. We have been commissioned to bring people into the presence of God and everything else flows from there. We even invented a word to describe what has been happening for decades: *unchurched.*

The *unchurched* are the people who are not part of the church we have been building and the primary task of most pastors, leaders and disciples over my lifetime has been to connect the unchurched to the church. That sounds right, doesn't it? No! Not even close.

The primary focus of millions of Christians across the world for many decades has been to fulfil a mandate that God never gave us! At no point in history have we been called by God to connect the unchurched to the church!

How embarrassing is it to admit that so much of the energy of the church which bears the name of Christ has been devoted to fulfilling an assignment which Christ never gave us?

Not only did Jesus never call us to lead the unchurched to the Church – I doubt Jesus would understand or accept our terminology. I doubt we even really understand it!

What does *unchurched* mean? When we do lead an *unchurched* person into the church, does that mean they are now *churched*? That's not even a word and nor is *unchurched*, if we really want to be honest. Someone just made up the word many years ago so as to enable us to categorise people in the world as those who are 'in' and those who are 'out' and we embraced the role of those who were called to lead them into the church. We then had the audacity to say that this was what God called us to do!

We need to forget all that gibberish and listen to what the Spirit of God is saying to the people of God today and every day. We are called to lead people to a Person with Whom they will have a relationship which will forever transform their life.

Our calling is to then disciple those people so they may grow closer to God, in Christ, through Christ and for Christ.

This was the Apostle Paul's calling and it was his prayer for everyone to whom he ministered. Paul's prayer in Ephesians 3 is full of the language of intimacy, the language of relationship. Paul led people into a personal encounter with a living God in Christ. Paul never built a church – Jesus did that.

> *"I pray that out of his glorious riches he may strengthen you with power through his Spirit in your inner being, so that Christ may dwell in your hearts through faith. And I pray that you, being rooted and established in love, may have power, together with all the Lord's holy people, to grasp how wide and long and high and deep is the love of Christ, and to know this love that surpasses knowledge – that you may be filled to the measure of all the fullness of God.*
>
> *Now to him who is able to do immeasurably more than all we ask or think, according to his power that is at work within us, to him be glory in the church and in Christ Jesus throughout all generations, for ever and ever! Amen."*
> *(Ephesians 3:16-21)*

Therefore, in that most prayed prayer of all time, the model prayer Jesus gave us, we declare, *"Your kingdom come, Your will be done on earth as it is in heaven,"* and then we notice that the rest of this amazing prayer that Jesus gave us, actually contains the *fruit* of that first prayer.

By that I mean this: when the Kingdom of heaven comes; when the reality of the Kingdom heaven is birthed in the kingdom of this world, then God will give us our daily bread; our sins will be forgiven; we will then be empowered to forgive others; He will strengthen us in temptation and He will deliver us from evil. When we pray (or declare), *"Your Kingdom Come,"* everything else flows from that reality and that is when *"as it is in heaven"* then becomes our new daily reality. Hallelujah! Bring it on, Lord!

Now I have always encouraged people to pray about anything and everything. Some people have a very long list of things and people to pray about and that's great. God loves to hear our prayers and see our faith as we pray. But the mother and father of all prayers, if I can put it that way is, *"Your Kingdom Come."* Then the next phrase, *"Your will be done on earth as it is in heaven,"* is actually the fruit of and the answer to, *"Your Kingdom Come."*

We need to grasp this simple truth: **when God's kingdom invades the kingdom of this earth, God's will is always done on earth as it is in heaven.**

So, in anticipation of where God wants to take us on this exciting Kingdom adventure, let me give you a clear statement of purpose for yourself, for me and for the church Jesus promised to build. This is our calling and our commission. Each and every day, this is what we should be doing:

> *'Touching heaven, changing earth,*
> *in Christ, through Christ, for Christ.'*

That is our assignment from God, our purpose, our reason for being here. Every day, in every possible way, we are called by God to release heaven on earth. That was and is the mission of Christ and He has called us to partner with Him in His mission.

When God came into our world in the flesh as Jesus of Nazareth, heaven was opened and every day of His life, as well as through His death and resurrection, Jesus touched heaven and changed the earth. Every sermon, every healing, every miracle, every action by Jesus was evidence of the coming Kingdom. Everywhere Jesus during His ministry, He declared, *"The Kingdom of heaven is at hand,"* or *"the Kingdom of heaven is among you,"* or *"the Kingdom of heaven is within you."*

Jesus spoke about the Kingdom of Heaven constantly. Then before leaving us in the flesh, Jesus said an amazing thing to His disciples, and then and to us today through the Holy Spirit. He said:

> "As I have been sent, so I am sending you' and then He breathed on them and said, 'receive the Holy Spirit."
> (John 20:21,22)

What happened next? The Kingdom of heaven exploded across the community and God's will and purpose unfolded in truly spectacular ways - as it is in heaven! Jesus was building His church with an effectiveness and a power that we only dream of seeing today.

So how did those early disciples trigger such an explosion? It's simple really. **They never tried to do God's job.** They were fully aware at every moment of every day that it was the power of God through His emerging Kingdom presence which would change the world.

Their assignment was to speak the truth about Jesus and allow the Spirit of God to use the word of their testimony (Revelation 12:11) to demolish strongholds and lead people to Christ. Jesus did the rest, just as He promised He would.

So, strap yourself in. That's where we are headed in this book. The mission of Christ has not changed. The calling of God on the lives of His people has not changed. Our purpose in still being here and the God-given responsibility placed on every disciple is the same as it always has been.

We are called to advance the Kingdom of heaven, by His grace, for His glory as stewards of His presence and authority, in the power of the Holy Spirit.

Are you brave enough to boldly pray and declare, *"Your Kingdom Come!"* and not stop until God answers?

Are you ready for God to completely transform you and those around you as He answers that prayer, so that your life is finally lived and experienced as it is in heaven?

Don't respond too quickly here - because saying 'yes' may very well open the floodgates of heaven and you will need to learn very quickly how to surf that mighty wave in faith and trust God to lead you deeper into Him as you learn to embrace your God-given destiny in Christ, through Christ and for Christ.

CHAPTER TWO
Heaven Has Come to Earth

I began this book by making a somewhat bold assertion which you may be wrestling with still. I was presumptuous enough to tell you why you are here. I said that you and I and all those who claim to be disciples of Jesus Christ are here for the same reason. Then as the logical extension of that assertion I suggested that the same reason is therefore the primary purpose of the Christian church across the whole world.

You and I and all believers are part of the Church which the Lord Jesus Christ promised to build and as such we have been called, commissioned and empowered by God to do one thing primarily – and that one thing happens to be the mission of Christ and the very reason He came to earth.

Jesus came to release heaven on earth and He has called us to join Him in that mission.

That is why in the model prayer Jesus gave His followers, there's an essential declaration from which the title of this book has been drawn. Jesus told us to pray and declare:

> *"Your Kingdom come, Your will be done on earth as it is in heaven." (Matthew 6:10)*

We must understand that this was not some nice, philosophical, flowery prayer to inspire and soothe people who were in trouble. This was a powerful apostolic commission! This was (and is) our assignment on earth, and all of heaven is backing this prayer each and every day and anticipating its fulfilment.

We should be compelled to pray and declare, *"Your Kingdom come..."* and then help make that happen.

This is not an optional task if we are a true disciple of Christ wanting to embrace the mission of Christ. This assignment lies at the absolute centre of who we are in Christ. It's lies at the absolute centre of why God has left you and me on this planet - because God has wonderful plans for this place and we are a vital part of those plans.

Tragically however, too much of the church's theology and focus during my lifetime has been wrapped up in the dysfunction of this world and its ultimate demise. Many Christians actually get this strange, perhaps even perverted sense of encouragement when disaster happens. Have you noticed this? There is a weird sense of affirmation that comes upon some people in a crisis or when a tragic event occurs because they believe 'the end is near.' The end of what? Are we disciples of Jesus Christ or not?

There is no 'end' to His Kingdom and our purpose is to advance His Kingdom on earth! So why would anyone who claims to embrace Christ's mission, be focused on anything other than the advancement of His Kingdom and leading people to Him? Why would any disciple of Jesus want to re-arm Satan by focussing on what's wrong in our world? That is exactly what we are doing when we allow our minds and hearts to be captured by anything other than the mission of Christ and advancing His Kingdom.

Let me ask you: Who did God put in charge? Let me ask that again: Who did God put in charge? It's an easy answer: Jesus. So how did Jesus model dealing with storms? How did Jesus model dealing with disease? What did Jesus do to confront the deep corruption of His day? How did Jesus transform humanity and bring about change? Was it by focussing on people's sin? Was it by campaigning against the moral decay in society? Was it by pointing out what is wrong with the world? Was it by preaching doom and gloom to an already broken people? No!

Jesus Christ modelled something for us that is as simple as it is profound. Jesus spent His days among us on earth doing one thing primarily: Releasing the reality of God's world into this world. That was His mission and that, my friends, is also our divine assignment – releasing heaven on earth. That's at the core of who we are.

Everything we do, every day of our lives, either contributes to that outcome or it takes us and others away from that outcome – there's no middle ground. Our assignment is to release the reality of God's perfect Kingdom of light and life and liberty, into the brokenness, dysfunction and darkness of this earthly kingdom.

Every moment of every day we walk upon this earth, that is our assignment - to bring a new reality into this world, as it is in heaven! That is the lifestyle to which God has called us. My job and your job every day is to release heaven on earth.

Now in saying that, I need to address the main problem we have had in understanding this reality. For too long I believe we have focused on our destination and neglected the mission of Christ here and now. Our destination is clear – we will dwell only in the Kingdom of heaven! Praise God! But our God-given assignment is to bring heaven to earth first.

The Kingdom of heaven is not just a destination we go to in the future – it is actually a spiritual domain which transcends time and space - as distinct from the physical domain of this earth which had a beginning and it will have an end.

The Kingdom of heaven is the King's domain. Hence the word king-dom. It's the realm of the King's dominion and that King is Jesus. Yes, there will be a time when the only Kingdom we know will be the Kingdom of heaven. But until then, we live in two kingdoms.

George Eldon Ladd penned a phrase years ago in one of his books which beautifully describes the Kingdom of heaven from our perspective now. He said it is *'the presence of the future.'*

There is definitely a future aspect of the Kingdom of heaven and the day will surely come when we are only part of that Kingdom, unencumbered by this bag of bones and this broken world.

That is our destiny - eternal life in the eternal Kingdom to which God has called us in Christ - and don't we long for that day? Just look at the number of hymns and worship songs that have been written and sung which focus our hearts on that future, glorious reality of dwelling only in the kingdom of heaven!

Sadly however, far less attention has been given to the present reality of the Kingdom of heaven. *'The presence of the future'* is a perfect description of where we live right now. It also explains why Jesus came to earth and what He did when He got here. He brought the future into the present; He removed the veil between heaven and earth and that is still His mission, through us.

Jesus came into a kingdom where Satan had wreaked havoc for thousands of years. He gave up the glory of heaven and stepped into the womb of a frightened teenage girl and become one with humanity. Why?

There are lots of reasons and some pretty important theology to understand in answering that fully, but for now, I will give you just one of the reasons Jesus became human. He came to show us what a fully alive human being, in touch with the Kingdom of heaven, can do in this midst of this broken, fallen world. He came to release the power, the reality and the fruitfulness of the Kingdom of heaven into the kingdom of this world.

Then, before Jesus left this world, He stood before humanity as a man, as one of us, and He made a statement that we really need to understand. We read it in Matthew 28 where Jesus said, *"All authority has been given to me ..."*

This is Jesus, the Son of God, Who became the Son of man. He laid aside all that He had in heaven – which was actually everything that exists – because He owned it all. He loosened His grip on all that to become a man.

But then through His perfect life, His atoning death and His glorious resurrection, Jesus re-inherited everything *as a man*, so that you and I, as fellow-humans in Him, could now share in that inheritance.

Then this man, Jesus, stood among us after His triumphant resurrection, having defeated the power of death, and He said to all humanity, *"I got the keys to heaven back. All that you lost in the garden - I got it back! Now, let's get back to 'Plan A' shall we? Because, all authority has been given to me, in heaven and on earth."*

Now it's really important for us to understand that Jesus did not make that declaration as God. Jesus is God incarnate in His essence but He made that statement as a man. We know that because He said, *"All authority has been given to me."*

There is no one higher than God who can give God anything. So, when Jesus made that statement, He was speaking as a man - as our brother – as one just like us!

So let me ask you another question. If Jesus can say, as a man, as our brother, as the Son of Man, *"All authority has been given to me,"* how much authority does that leave Satan? Zero!

Jesus has been given **all** authority in heaven and on earth and that means Satan has no authority!

Now the Devil certainly has power and he has the ability to inflict all manner of evil in this world, but for that to be effective against the church, Satan needs to get his authority somewhere other than God because God has given all authority to Jesus.

So where do you think Satan gets his authority from now? He gets his authority from us when we come into agreement with him. That's exactly what happened in the garden of Eden. We came into agreement with Satan when we believed his lie and when you believe the lie, you empower the liar.

The more that happens - the more we see the kingdom of this world falling apart; the more you focus on what is wrong in the world – the worse it becomes! If you focus on the darkness - the darkness grows. We already know that the only way to dispel darkness is to turn up the light.

So, our calling in Christ, Who is the Light of the world, is to switch on that light, every opportunity we get, which, in this context means we release on earth the power of the Kingdom of heaven and the presence of the King! That's our assignment. It's not complicated. Jesus made this very simple with these words: *"As the Father has sent me, I am sending you. The assignment I have is the assignment I give to you. Now go and release heaven on earth."*

It seems that horrible things are continually taking place. We live in a broken, dysfunctional world. But you shouldn't concentrate on the negative and the problems; instead, you should always concentrate on the solution. Jesus Christ is the solution and the more His Kingdom comes, the more God's purpose will be fulfilled! What we humans focus on the most will become a part of us. We also tend to become like the people we spend time with. The people we look up to and want to be like are the people we tend to follow.

The Kingdom of heaven should be your primary concern; you should spend more time with Jesus than with anybody else, and you should strive to live in Him, through Him, and for Him. When that happens, your life and the world around you will be completely transformed.

Some people go through life trapped in the book of Job, rather than being set free by the Gospels and the book of Acts. In a world where Satan is successful in his objective and we are still looking for a saviour, the narrative of Job will demonstrate how terrible this world can become. But I am not a disciple of Job. I am a disciple of Jesus. I live this side of the cross. The Saviour has already come!

Job was the question - Jesus is the answer. If you study the life of Job and it does not lead you to Jesus, then you have never really understood the question, and you will most definitely miss the answer. In actual fact, if you study any part of the Old Testament and it does not bring you to Jesus, then you have completely missed the message of the Bible. It is all about Jesus and the Kingdom that He is establishing among us.

The majority of Christians, however, base their faith on what God has not yet accomplished. When I've done that throughout my life; when I focus on what has not happened yet, I create the perfect atmosphere for Satan to plant his seeds of doubt and discouragement. We should always be focusing on what God has already accomplished and promised as His Kingdom comes and His will is done on earth as it is in heaven.

If we do not make this our primary emphasis each day, we will invariably begin to develop a concept of God that is founded on disappointment rather than revelation. There is already a clear answer to every question which we will ever have concerning God: His name is Jesus.

In terms of theology, Jesus Christ is perfect theology. Whatever it is that you are unable to discover in Jesus Christ is not worth knowing. Jesus is the person through whom God has spoken to us and revealed His character, His heart, and His plan.

We are given the responsibility of representing Christ in the manner in which He actually is. To put it another way, when God made it possible for the Spirit who raised Jesus from the dead to reside within us, that rendered helplessness inexcusable! This side of the cross, helplessness is completely unjustifiable, but also totally intolerable in a disciple of Christ.

You and I are both filled with the Holy Spirit, the same Spirit Who brought Jesus back from the dead, and He desires to flow through us and bring about a change in the world around us. He is not in us as a lake; rather, He is in us as a river. Rivers are a source of life as they move and flow. God released a river of life within you when you were born again, and there are times when all you need to do is believe in your own conversion and allow God to carry out what He had planned to do in you and through you. This is what happened when you were born again.

When I listen to the prayers of others, and even my own prayers at times, I have come to the realisation that we continue to pray for things that we already possess. God has already provided everything we ever need, and yet we continue to pray for more of those things.

We are perplexed as to why we become disinterested in praying; the reason is that we are focusing our attention on things that we already have. We form the impression that God is not answering those petitions, but in truth, He has already answered them; we have simply failed to walk in the power and the reality of those answers He has already given us!

There is a spirit of wisdom and revelation that is being released across the church in these troubled times, and I believe that this spirit will cause us to actually rise up and become who God says we already are. I cannot allow myself to entertain any thoughts about myself that are not already God's thoughts about me.

This is exactly what Paul meant when he said in the first few verses of the third chapter of Colossians, "*Since, then, you have been raised with Christ, set your hearts on things above, where Christ is, seated at the right hand of God.*"

It is of the utmost importance that we fill our minds with those things that the Holy Spirit can affirm with a resounding "*Amen!*" Your mind is an extremely valuable part of you. In order to safeguard your thoughts, Jesus Christ had to die. He places a very high value on your mind.

On the other hand, the mind is really only a blessing when it is subjected to the influence of the Spirit of God. In order to educate us how to think, Jesus wants to teach us to have a Kingdom perspective. He wants to teach us how to think like someone who already lives in His Kingdom.

I believe Jesus wants to establish a revival culture that fosters an environment in which anything can take place at any time. Our mission is not to get people into an organisation; it is to bring the Kingdom of heaven into every part of our life and our world.

A heavenly mission was given to you the instant you embraced the Kingdom of heaven. This assignment became yours when you were born again. Along with that duty comes a desire to accomplish things that are unachievable.

Because it is a part of who you are, you should not be satisfied until you witness the power of God at work in you and in the world around you.

We all have many goals, dreams and aspirations. We all have accomplishments in life - things take place in our life that are very encouraging and affirming to us. When we have witnessed an impossibility bow down to the name of Jesus, however, we have witnessed the thing that truly stays with us the longest. That stuff doesn't die. It's why in Psalm 145 we read this: *"the works of the Lord will praise Him."* The works of the Lord are like living entities that declare God's greatness whenever they are repeated.

I want to remind you of one of the most incredible statements that can be found in the Bible as I wrap up this chapter. You will find it in the gospel of John. Jesus is speaking and He says this:

> *"Very truly I tell you, the Son can do nothing by himself; he can do only what he sees his Father doing, because whatever the Father does the Son also does." (John 5:19)*

It is Jesus, the man, who is speaking and He is saying, *"I cannot heal the sick; I cannot raise the dead; I cannot multiply food; I cannot bring the Kingdom of Heaven down to earth on my own. I am unable to perform any of the miracles that I am famous for. I am unable to do it. I can only participate in what I see the Father doing."*

So, what exactly is going on in this situation? Despite the fact that Jesus was eternally God, He decided to spend His life on earth under the constraints of being a man. He chose to lay aside His heavenly powers and become one of us. Why? So that He might serve as an example for us to follow.

If Jesus were to accomplish all of His miracles as God, I would still be impressed, but I would not feel obliged to follow in His footsteps because that would be God at work, and I am not God. I would simply take a step back and exclaim, *"Wow, that is truly incredible! Do some more, God - that's awesome!"*

It is when I come to the realisation that Jesus chose to display what life is like for any human being who is empowered by the Spirit of God, then He becomes a true role-model – Someone in Whose footsteps I can follow. The life that Jesus exemplifies is essentially the typical Christian life.

Although Jesus was not considered a Christian in the strictest sense, He did, without a doubt, serve as a model for what all Christians ought to be like and how they ought to spend their lives as they follow in His footsteps. He demonstrated what is possible for every believer who takes a step forward in faith, empowered by the Holy Spirit, and embraces His purpose on earth, which is to bring heaven to earth.

This chapter contains some sizable chunks of spiritual meat, so I would encourage you to read it again and make sure you get a firm grasp of what I have just shared with you before moving on.

Kingdom of God, come! Will of God, be done, on earth as it is in heaven!

CHAPTER THREE
The Gate is Open!

"Now Jacob went out from Beersheba and went toward Haran. So, he came to a certain place and stayed there all night, because the sun had set. And he took one of the stones of that place and put it at his head, and he lay down in that place to sleep. Then he dreamed, and behold, a ladder was set up on the earth, and its top reached to heaven; and there the angels of God were ascending and descending on it ... (to v.16) Then Jacob awoke from his sleep and said, 'Surely the Lord is in this place and I did not know it.'"
(Genesis 28:10–13,16)

Before we take a look Jacob's experience with God in this story, I would like to discuss the final sentence first: *'Surely the Lord is in this place and I did not know it.'* I remember several years ago I printed those words on a piece of paper and stuck them on the top of the pulpit where I preached every week.

I also printed them on little pieces of paper and distributed them to all of the members of the congregation. I requested that they place them in their bibles, on their refrigerators, or in a location that was easily visible. I wanted us to be reminded on a regular basis that we have the potential to overlook the Lord even while He is working in our midst!

In the course of my ministry, I have witnessed this many times. I might be preaching and I can see the Holy Spirit transforming people from the inside out as the Lord ministers to them in a wonderful way, but in the midst of that, I see another person who is more likely thinking about what they will eat for lunch or whether or not they will arrive home in time to watch the football game. How can that happen? Such different responses.

The Holy Spirit of God certainly operates differently in different individuals and at different times, and because of this, it is not unusual to witness some people being impacted more than others. However, I am not talking about that specific dynamic here. In this context, I am referring to our constant and all-encompassing knowledge of the Lord.

When it is very evident that God is at work among us, how is it that we can become so disconnected? I believe that God is always working among us, even though the majority of the time we are unaware of it. Why do we miss Him so often?

As someone who has worked in front-line ministry for more than four decades, I believe I finally have the answer. There is a direct correlation between our hunger and our desire for God and the degree to which we are aware of the Kingdom of heaven and the work that the Lord is doing in our midst and even in our own hearts and lives.

It is not a complicated matter; it is simply the way that we people function. When one is hungry, perception is enhanced, and when one is not hungry, perception is hindered.

So be warned: **In the Kingdom of heaven, you will rarely fine what you're not hungry for.**

"Surely the Lord is in this place, and I did not know it." Why was I unaware of it? It was simply because I was not looking for the Lord. I was not focussed on God and His kingdom. I was not hungry for His presence and His active involvement in what was happening in me and around me. Hunger helps perception.

Why do you think the prostitutes, the tax collectors and the wicked people in Jesus' day all knew who He was?

They were aware of their need and had a hunger for change. By contrast, the religious leaders were completely oblivious to the situation since they were content with the knowledge and religious power that thought they possessed.

As a result of their lack of awareness of their own personal needs, they did not seek God. They were unable to satisfy their need for Him, and as a result, they were unable to perceive His presence, even while He was standing directly in front of them in Jesus!

On the other hand, even the most heinous of sinners that existed throughout the time of Jesus and continue to exist today are aware of the fact that they need something different in their lives and their hunger enhances their ability to see into the Kingdom.

We can pray "*Your kingdom come*" as much as we want, but unless that prayer is accompanied by a hunger; a profound yearning; a longing for God's real presence and power in our lives, in our families, in our church and nation, we won't see the Kingdom of heaven unleashed around us.

Let's go back to Genesis 28.

> *(Jacob said) "Surely the Lord is in this place and I did not know it." And he was afraid and said, "How awesome is this place! This is none other than the house of God, and this is the gate of heaven!"*
>
> *(Then to verse 19). And he called the name of that place Bethel ..."* *(And 'Bethel' means 'house of God.')*
> *(Genesis 28:16,19)*

Now this expression that Jacob uses, "*The House of God,*" is cited in the Bible on multiple occasions and in a variety of different settings. The phrase "*The House of God*" appears for the very first time in the Bible right here.

It is referred to as a "house," however there is no actual building. Of course, we already know now that the building is not the house of God - the people are the dwelling place of the Spirit of God - <u>we</u> are the house of God. But in this verse, there's no building or people. There's just one guy sleeping on a rock and when he discovers God is there he exclaims, *"This is awesome . . this is God's house!"* But the thing that I want you to really grasp here is his description of the house of God. He says, *"This is none other than the house of God, this is the gate of heaven."*

The gate of heaven – the portal to paradise! All of us are aware of what a gate is. A gate is a place of transition. We have a gate at our house that allows us to move from the backyard to the front yard whenever we want to. Maybe there is a gate at your house which allows you to move from your back yard to a public reserve that is located behind your house.

A gate is therefore a transition place where you go from one realm to another. The Bible describes the house of God as a gate – but not just any gate – this is the gate of heaven. So, let's take a moment to go back in time – all the way back!

In the beginning, before the creation of man, there was a fall in heaven. As a result of Lucifer's insatiable need to be worshipped, he was expelled from heaven, and he found himself on earth. When all is said and done, the planet itself becomes the dominion or kingdom over which Satan rules.

At this point, it is essential that we comprehend that Satan is the ruler of this world, that's how he is depicted in the Bible on numerous occasions. In 1 John 5 we are told that the power of the devil is over the entire world.

You will recall that Satan presented Jesus with all of the kingdoms of this world when he faced Him in the wilderness at the beginning of His ministry.

That was something Satan could only do if they were his to give away. Consequently, Satan has been in control of this world almost from the very beginning, long before the creation of mankind. In the book of Job, Satan challenged God, and the conversation that ensued began with God asking Satan, *"Where have you come from?"* Satan responded by saying, *"From going to and fro on the earth, and from walking up and down on it."* (Job 1:7). Peter draws on this image here:

> *"Be sober minded; be watchful, Your adversary the devil roams the earth like a roaring lion, seeking someone to devour." (1 Peter 5:8)*

This verse was written many years after the original passage. So, right in the centre of this kingdom of darkness; in the middle of Satan's domain, God planted a garden because He desired to raise up a people who were created in His image; who were worshippers by choice and who would overthrow this fallen earthly kingdom.

All of that serves as the background for this passage in Genesis, in which we have this image of the house of God as the gate of heaven. Through this gate angels are able to ascend and descend. When they ascend, it is because they have completed a task, and when they descend, it is because they have been assigned a new task to complete in God's mission to overthrow and destroy the ruler of this world.

This picture of the house of God is important to us. Every one of the 'houses of God' that are mentioned in the Bible served a very important function. They illustrated something. For instance, the presence of the Lord was said to have rested on the Tabernacle of Moses. Contrary to what some people believe, the Tabernacle of Moses was not a representation of the church. It was actually a depiction of Jesus, Who would one day come to earth to die for the world and establish the church.

It featured an altar for the offering of sacrifices, the washing of water, the Word of God, the candlestick, the showbread (Jesus is the bread of life and the light of the world), incense, and the great intercessor, among other things. It was clear that Jesus was the one in question.

The 'house' that talked about you and me is this one here in Genesis 28, but there is no description whatsoever other than to state that God was present, and wherever God is present, the Kingdom of heaven is present. That is, wherever God is present, there is an 'open heaven.' This brings to mind the words of the Apostle John in his gospel:

> "And the Word became flesh and dwelt among us, and we beheld His glory, the glory of the only begotten of the Father, full of grace and truth." (John 1:14)

Jesus Christ, the Word of God, became a man and lived among us. This is simply incredible. Jesus Christ, the Word of God, took on human form and dwelt among us. The word *dwelt* in this context literally translates as *tabernacled*.

It might be understood that the Word of God took on flesh and became a tabernacle among us. God's dwelling place is the tabernacle, which in the original context was a building or structure. But what about now? Stay with me here - this is really significant.

I am sure you are aware of the fact that the Holy Spirit resided within Jesus when He was on earth. The heavens opened while Jesus was being baptised, and the Holy Spirit came upon Him and remained on Him from that point on. But I wonder if you ever thought about the fact that during those three and half years of Jesus' earthly ministry, the Holy Spirit did not live in anybody else on the planet. He couldn't because no one was born again. Only Jesus was without sin, so the Spirit of God lived in Him and rested upon Him.

Jesus would later describe this to the disciples when He said, " ... *the Holy Spirit that is with you will be in you."* (John 14:17). He's referring to the fact that the Spirit of God would be abiding with them, to help direct them, to empower their ministry, but the Spirit was not yet residing in them. That could not happen until their sin was atoned for - which couldn't happen until Jesus died. Let me jump towards the end of John 1. At this point in time Jesus is the house of God, the dwelling place of God on the earth, and He has this encounter with a guy named Nathaniel:

> *"Jesus saw Nathanael coming toward Him, and said of him, "Behold, an Israelite indeed, in whom is no deceit!" Nathanael said to Him, "How do You know me?" Jesus answered and said to him, "Before Philip called you, when you were under the fig tree, I saw you." (John 1:47)*

Jesus experiences a vision, a word of knowledge, in which the Holy Spirit reveals to Him a man seated beneath a tree. This is what He conveys to Nathaniel. Obviously, Nathaniel is going to pay attention to this, as you can probably understand.

> *"Nathanael answered and said to Him, "Rabbi, You are the Son of God! You are the King of Israel! Jesus answered and said to him, "Because I said to you, 'I saw you under the fig tree,' do you believe? You will see greater things than these." And He said to him, "Most assuredly, I say to you, hereafter you shall see heaven open, and the angels of God ascending and descending upon the Son of Man." (John 1:49)*

What did the Genesis 'House of God' have? An open heaven with angels of God ascending and descending and the voice of the Lord came forth. It was the manifest abiding presence of God in that location. What did Jesus have? The same thing, an open heaven, angels ascending and descending and the voice of the Father. Why?

Because the house of God is the gate of heaven. It is the gate between two worlds, two kingdoms, the gate that allows one kingdom to influence the other. If we choose to live each day with a deep awareness of this fact, then we will be able to partner with the Lord in His work in a far more intentional manner.

Consequently, we are currently living in a state of perpetual conflict or tension - caught between the Kingdom of heaven and the kingdom of this world, which are simultaneously existing realities. The most important question we must face then is: where is your primary engagement?

If the kingdom of this world is the centre of your attention each day, then the Kingdom of heaven will, at most, be a blur in the background.

If, on the other hand, you have the Kingdom of heaven constantly as your primary focus, then the way in which you live, move, and have your being in this earthly kingdom will be profoundly impacted, as will those around you.

Jacob uttered those words during the very first glimpse that we have of our mission on earth: *"This is the house of God – the gate of heaven."* Centuries later, on this side of the cross of Christ, *we* are the House of God — *we* are the gate of heaven.

If you choose to live each day with that reality foremost in your mind and your heart, it will impact the way you think and the choices you make.

You will always promote and live in the reality of the kingdom that you are most aware of and most focused upon.

Jesus lived His life with the realisation of an infinite supply from the Kingdom of heaven because He was focussing His attention on a reality that has no limits or limitations.

Taking inspiration from that environment was what made it possible for Him to respond to every situation with a solution and a response.

Jesus became the gate of heaven, and then He handed that baton to you and me. Jesus was the embodiment of the picture that God had given to Jacob all those years ago.

In the third chapter of Colossians the Apostle Paul nails this idea when he says, *"We are seated in heavenly places in Christ."* What Jesus did for you and for me was to clear the way so that we are now without excuse. Because we live as a gate, we now have access to the King and His Kingdom, and we do not have to go through any hardships or exert a great deal of effort to do so.

We have unrestricted access to the King and His Kingdom at any time of the day or night. This is because we are able to bring the reality of His realm into this realm, releasing heaven on earth.

As you continue to concentrate on the reality of the Kingdom of heaven, you will be able to release the rule of the King in this world to a greater extent. Your ability to bring that power, that victory, and that reality into your world, into your nation, into your community, into your church, into your family, and into your life will increase to the degree to which you are able to focus on what Jesus Christ has already secured for you in the Kingdom of heaven.

Having said that, here is the knockout blow in all of this. Jesus comes into the world as a human being, and He is the house of God, the dwelling place of God on earth. However, He then does something quite outrageous. He then turns to each of us and says, *"Tag, you're in. You are now the house of God!"* He says, *"I am the light of the world,"* then He says, *"You are the light of the world."*

He does all these amazing things everywhere He goes and then says, *"Even greater things than this will you do!"* He passes the baton to his people and says *"Here, my assignment is now your assignment. As the Father has sent me - I am sending you."*

Now, there is a lot to think about in this chapter, so I want to encourage you to go back and spend some time working through it again, stopping where you need to as you allow the Holy Spirit to answer your questions and provide you with a much clearer understanding of who you are in Christ and how you ought to live as a citizen of these two kingdoms and as the gate between those kingdoms.

Let me just recap as I finish this chapter:

- Genesis 28 - Jacob is asleep on a rock and God shows up. Jacob declares, *"This is the house of God, the gate of heaven."* Without knowing it, he foreshadows what is to come.

- Isaiah 64 – the people of God cry out day after day, *"Oh that you would rend (tear open) the heavens and come down."*

- Almost a thousand years later, Jesus steps out of heaven into the womb of a Jewish teenager and becomes human. When it was time for His Kingdom ministry to begin, God answered that prayer from Isaiah 64.

    As Jesus rose from the waters of baptism, heaven was torn open and the Spirit of God, the presence of God descended upon Jesus and remained on Him, <u>as a man</u>, throughout His whole ministry.

- For the first time in human history, the Kingdom of heaven was opened to the kingdom of this world and it remained open from that day forward. For the first time in history the presence of God 'tabernacled' or dwelt within a human being.

- Jesus then spent the next three and half years releasing the Kingdom of heaven on earth. Wherever He went, the reality of heaven broke loose on earth. The sick were healed, the lost were found, the dead were raised, the blind could see, the deaf could hear, the lame could dance. What was true in heaven became true on earth as Jesus, the gate of heaven, allowed that reality to spill into this reality.

- Then when Jesus completed His mission with His death and resurrection, He stood before humanity and said, *"Tag, you're in!"* Well, what He actually said was, *"As the Father has sent me, so I am sending you."* Then He breathed on us and said, *"Receive the Holy Spirit."*

- Now we have the presence of God and the mission of Christ. We are called, commissioned and empowered to be the gate of heaven on earth. Now it is <u>us</u> who can say, *"Surely the Lord is in this place and I did not know it."*

CHAPTER FOUR
In His Presence

Jesus provided us with a model prayer and encouraged us to pray saying, "*Your kingdom come, your will be done on earth as it is in heaven.*" However, what does it look like when that petition is answered? What does it really mean to be a citizen of this broken, dysfunctional earthly kingdom while simultaneously living in the Kingdom of heaven? What kind of lifestyle do we live after we are entirely devoted to Jesus? Heaven operates in a manner that is completely different to that of earth; therefore, what is it like to reside in what the New Testament refers to as the Kingdom of God or the Kingdom of heaven?

These questions are important to us all because one of the key responsibilities that has been placed upon us as believers is to get an understanding of how God's Kingdom operates. Heaven is a reality that exists in the current moment, something that can be perceived, comprehended, and experienced by us. It is intended that the Kingdom of heaven will have an effect on the way in which we perceive reality and the way in which we construct our value system. The more we embrace and experience this practical expression of the Kingdom of heaven and the more we learn how to structure and organise our lives around the basic ideals of that Kingdom, then the more transformational we will become as we impact this earthly kingdom.

I believe that this prayer Jesus gave us, is the most important representation of the heartbeat of Jesus for our lives. This is His heart's desire for each of us – that we will radically impact the world around us as we live out His mission on earth – a mission which can be summed up in the words: "*Your kingdom come, Your will be done on earth, as it is in heaven.*"

When Jesus told us to pray this it wasn't just a pipe dream or a plan to keep us spiritually minded and occupied until He comes back. This was a strategic military assignment in the war against God's enemy - the ruler of this broken world. In point of fact, it is included in the category of prayers offered by apostles.

So, what exactly is an apostolic prayer? To begin, the name *apostle* literally means *sent one*, but it encompasses a great deal more than that. In the Roman army, it was common practice to dispatch a military commander to a territory that had already been conquered. This is where the concept behind this word originated. They would send this military leader in along with a group of architects, language specialists, and other specialists that were necessary to re-design the appearance of this city or occasionally even a whole nation.

They were commissioned to redesign the roads, the way the cities functioned, the principles that they used in commerce, and to teach the people the language of Rome. They continued doing all of this until the city actually looked and functioned like Rome. Why? So as to ensure that the Emperor would have a sense of comfort when he arrived.

When Jesus instructs His followers to pray "*on earth as it is in heaven,*" they are referring to the apostolic prayer. This is where the challenge that we face rests. Is it even feasible for us to have homes, churches, cities, and even nations in which Jesus feels at home? Places that function like the kingdom in which He has dwelt for eternity? It must be because that is our assignment!

We need to understand that, *"on earth as it is in heaven"* is not some waffly philosophical concept, it's an apostolic directive to bring heaven to earth and to transform our surroundings so that this world functions like Jesus' world.

The reality of heaven then progressively becomes the reality of this world. That is our mission and our calling. That is the only reason we're here!

Now that we have accepted the task that Christ has given us and the calling that we have, it is of the utmost importance that we comprehend that everything in heaven is tied to one thing, and that is the presence of God. In heaven, the presence of God is the most significant reality and the most valuable thing there is. Because of this, we are not able to truly pray *"on earth as it is in heaven"* unless we are learning to recognize, value and embrace the presence of God.

To put it another way, this is not something that we can just pray for because we want to see cancer cured. It is not enough for us to just pray for the restoration of marriages or the success of businesses, because all of these things are suitable manifestations of heaven on earth. One of the most important aspects of the Kingdom of heaven is the presence of God. The central reality and dominant experience in the Kingdom of heaven is the presence of God Himself. He is everywhere and His presence has an effect everywhere.

In light of this fact, it is fascinating to observe that on Sundays, millions of people who are followers of God, congregate around a sermon in their respective locations all over the world. Despite the fact that they sing, worship, pray, and socialise with one another, the most important aspect of contemporary pastoral ministry is the preaching of the Word, also known as the sermon.

For a considerable amount of time, things have been like this. It is for this reason that the pulpit is elevated to a position that is high above everything else in many older church buildings and cathedrals. This is a representation of the importance of the Word of God as it is presented to us in sermons.

By contrast to that, if we look back in time and examine the people that God had gathered together, we can see that Israel gathered around the presence of God, and as a result, they were closer to experiencing the Kingdom of heaven than much of the current church is. Returning to those origins and that reality is necessary if we are serious about gaining a fuller understanding of how to really live in the Kingdom of heaven. To be tied to the one greatest value that is above all others, the presence of God, is something that we really need to learn.

It may be possible for us to learn how to live Kingdom lifestyles by merely studying principles. I can teach you certain principles about healing. I can teach you things to do when you face this sickness or that sickness, this condition that condition; what to do in this kind of church setting and what to do in that kind of church situation; what to do in public etc.

I can teach you the principles, and you may have some success. But if we want the full reality of, *"Yours is the kingdom, the power and the glory"* to break across our community and our nation then we need to follow the lead of Jesus.

The presence of God was at the core of Jesus' ministry. To say that principles are not significant is not accurate. You should look to principles whenever you are unable to recognise the presence of God. Although it is true that the Lord never abandons us, there are moments when He prevents us from being able to recognise Him, forcing us to behave in accordance with the principles that He has previously imparted to us.

Every one of us is on our own individual path of discovery. The absence of God's voice is never an indication of retribution. He is not disregarding us in any way.

He is simply aware that there are particular things that we will not discover unless He remains silent. However, God is always present, regardless of whether or not He is speaking directly to us.

> *"If I have told you earthly things, and you do not believe, how will you believe if I tell you heavenly things?" (John 3:12)*

Those words are spoken immediately after Jesus had informed Nicodemus that he needed to be born again. Having a child is a fairly natural process. So, Jesus is talking about something that everyone can relate to, and that is something that He is doing on purpose with Nicodemus.

When the Lord commences the process of revealing the essence of His world to us, He always begins with things that are within our comprehension. Consequently, Jesus discusses two worldly natural truths within the context of this discussion.

Despite the fact that he is talking about being reborn, He states in verse 8 that the wind blows wherever it pleases. Although you are able to hear its sound, you are unable to determine where it originates or where it is heading.

Therefore, He explains the nature of His world by using these natural realities of birth and the wind. This is the case with everyone who is born of the Spirit.

Throughout His mission, we find Jesus engaging in this activity on a regular basis - describing and explaining things that are in His reality, which is the Kingdom of heaven, by using things that we understand in our reality, the kingdom of this world. He teaches about sowing and reaping; He says the merciful will be blessed and will obtain mercy; you plant corn, you're going to harvest corn and the list goes on. He's teaching the nature of His world and how it connects to earthly principles and values.

In the Gospel of Matthew, we find an instruction that Jesus gave to all of His followers. Unfortunately, some Bible translations get this wrong. For example, here is the NIV translation:

> *"I will give you the keys of the kingdom of heaven; whatever you bind on earth will be [d] bound in heaven, and whatever you loose on earth will be [e] loosed in heaven."*
> *(Matthew 16:19)*

In this case, the translation is not accurate because it is just not possible to bind anything in time and then have it bound in eternity. Throughout the Bible, heaven serves as a model for the earth. That's why Jesus only did what He saw His Father doing. Everything He did was modelling heaven on planet earth.

Now the NIV translators acknowledge this with a footnote reference against the words *"will be."* If you read the footnote, it will give an alternate translation: *"will have been."*

According to this interpretation, the verse would therefore read as follows (which is the correct translation): *"Whatever you bind on earth will have been bound in heaven."* To expand that further, *"whatever you permit on earth will be what has already been permitted in heaven, and whatever you forbid on earth will be what has already been forbidden in heaven."* This is a translation of the verse that states that whatever you loose on earth will have already been loosed in heaven. The verse should therefore read:

> *"Whatever you bind on earth will have been bound in heaven. Whatever you loose on earth will have been loosed in heaven."*

So, all that to say this: heaven is the ultimate model. What is true in heaven can become true on earth as God's Kingdom comes and God's will is done on earth as it is in heaven.

The Bible tells us that the devil came to kill, steal and destroy. Wherever there's death, loss and destruction, we know the devil's fingerprints are present. But we also know that in the Kingdom of heaven the devil is a defeated enemy, a spent force and has no authority in heaven or on earth – because all authority has been given to Jesus. That's why we can bind sickness, oppression and all the fruits of darkness on earth, because they have already been bound in heaven.

Now the other portion of the command stipulates that whatever is loosed there must also be loosed here. But unless we get a clear revelation of His Kingdom, we don't know what to loose here!

You may remember the story that Jesus told in Luke 11:24 about the house being clean and swept and evil spirits driven out, and there was nothing put back in its place. So, the evil spirit came back seven times worse. The whole concept is when you displace you have to replace. So, when you bind, you've got to loose.

This may seem abstract, but from Jesus's perspective, this is just ministry 101. This is extremely practical. This is us becoming familiar with His world and releasing, or 'loosing' that reality into our world.

> *"No one has ascended to heaven, but he who came down from heaven, that is the son of man who is in heaven." (John 3:13)*

This verse is quite peculiar, so what does it actually mean? The earthly ministry of Jesus is just getting started at this point. It was three and a half years that He served as a minister and this was in the early days. This is where He introduces the concept of being born again. We therefore also know that the death, resurrection and ascension of Jesus is yet to talk place. In spite of this, Jesus stands before this group of people, and He declares, "*No one has ascended except for one.*"

Jesus is giving a description of His personal relationship with the Father. Now, I will admit that it's a little abstract, but Jesus is pointing us towards what we could call an ascended lifestyle. Which in layman's terms simply means our primary focus is on heaven. There is an assignment that has been given to us here.

'Going to heaven' is not my job. I certainly long for that day and will be overjoyed the day I am living only in that Kingdom. But that's not my assignment whilst I am on earth. My assignment (and yours) is to bring the reality of heaven here, now.

That's our mission because that is Christ's mission. It is not some abstract, unattainable, inconceivable goal that is out of reach. God gives all people who are born of the Spirit a military-like commission that is intensely practical. It is through Jesus Christ that He bestows upon them His authority and a flawless example of the life which they are to live: the life of Christ.

Therefore, when Jesus tells us that none has ascended to heaven except the One Who descended, He is casting light on His unique connection with the Father and that there is an ascension of sorts taking place for us. I don't fully comprehend it, but the text is there and we need to try and grasp the ungraspable!

Later on, the Apostle Paul was able to find a way to express this concept when he referred to it as *"being seated in heavenly places in Christ."*

One of the issues that we face is that Paul's statements are sometimes turned into dry and uninteresting doctrines rather than being invitations to a life-changing experience. To be able to understand doctrine and get the truth right is really important but that is never our goal. That is only the means to another end.

The truth is, there's no transformation without encounter and the transformation of a person never occurs just because they gained knowledge or insight. It comes because that insight led them to a Person. Jesus made this very clear when He said:

> *"You study the Scriptures diligently because you think that in them you have eternal life. These are the very Scriptures that testify about me, yet you refuse to come to me to have life." (John 5:39)*

The most important thing in the Kingdom of heaven is to have a personal encounter with God through Jesus Christ, as revealed by the Holy Spirit. As followers of Jesus, therefore, everything is tied to and flows from our relationship with God. Consequently, there is not a single aspect of our daily walk here in the kingdom of this world that is not in some way tied to our walk with Jesus in His heavenly Kingdom.

It is absolutely imperative that we never lose sight of the fact that the Kingdom of heaven is the realm of the King's domain, and that King is Jesus Christ. At all times, the King is present and presides over all of the activities which take place within His dominion. There is no way to discover and embrace the Kingdom of heaven if you do not have a connection to the King.

In the fourth chapter of John's gospel, we see Jesus speaking to the Samaritan woman at the well. In verse 23, Jesus states that the Father is looking for people who will *"worship Him in spirit and in truth."* It is important to note that the passage does not say that God is looking for worship. Rather than looking for worship, God is looking for those who worship Him. God is not an egotist who needs our approval in order to function. He's not insecure. He does not need us to tell Him He's doing a great job. God is looking for worshipers.

Why? Because He loves people and love always requires the best. There's nothing better God could want for you than for you to be a worshiper. Why? Because we always become like the one we worship!

So out of love for us, He leads us into the place of worship. We are drawn into a relationship with him. The presence of God beckons us because in His presence there is joy; in His presence there is freedom; in His presence there is victory; in His presence there is power; in His presence there is life; in His presence we find our identity, our calling, our purpose and our destiny; in His presence we see the reality of His kingdom; in His presence we become like Him. Paul captured all that perfectly here:

> *"Now the Lord is the Spirit, and where the Spirit of the Lord is, there is freedom. And we all, who with unveiled faces reflect the Lord's glory, are being transformed into his image with ever-increasing glory, which comes from the Lord, who is the Spirit." (2 Corinthians 3:17-18)*

I started this chapter by stating that we need to figure out how to be connected to the one thing that is of the utmost importance in the Kingdom of heaven, which is the presence of God. Paul explains the reason for this here. When we are in God's presence, we continually undergo a transformation into the image of Jesus Christ. In the presence of the Lord, we are a reflection of His glory. There is a direct correlation between the degree to which we accept the existence of heaven on earth and the degree to which we are then transformed into Christ's image. As we are transformed into the image of Jesus Christ, we reflect His glory and His light into the darkness of the world.

The next time there is a full moon, I encourage you to go outside at night and look at the moon and marvel at its beauty as the second most powerful natural light source in the universe.

If you live in a city, you may even want to get in your vehicle and drive out of town, away from the streetlights and any other sources of artificial light.

Once you reach your destination, park your vehicle, turn off the engine and lights, and then get out and just stand there and gaze at the moon. As you do, reflect on the fact that the moon is completely incapable of shining. That light is not coming from the moon.

The glow which illuminates the countryside all around you is actually the result of the sun's brightness being reflected off the moon and back towards you. The only time we are able to see everything so clearly in the darkness, is when the moon is able to capture the light from the sun. It would be impossible to see the moon if it did not reflect the glory of the sun.

"And we all, who with our faces uncovered reflect the glory of the Lord, are being transformed into his image with ever-increasing glory ..."

The only way we will be able to bring light into the darkness of this world is if we catch the glow that comes from the Son of God, Jesus, who is both our Lord and our Saviour. In the presence of the Lord, we are able to reflect the glory of the Lord with our faces unveiled, and this is only possible when we embrace His glorious presence.

The presence of God is the most important thing in the Kingdom of heaven. The degree to which we can recognise, acknowledge, and embrace His presence every day will determine the extent to which we are able to carry out the mission that Christ has given us here on earth.

This is a spiritual exercise. Jesus is present through His Spirit and it's too easy for us to ignore Him because He doesn't have skin on anymore!

I once asked a group of church leaders what they would say if Jesus walked into one of our worship services in the flesh. There was a long pause as they contemplated such an amazing event. Then one of my leaders was brutally honest and answered, *"Oops, You're real."*

Our greatest challenge in living in two kingdoms is the fact that one of them is only discerned spiritually. This earthly kingdom doesn't require much discernment. We are surrounded by things we can see, smell, hear, taste and touch. There's a little bit of mystery here and there but it's easy to live only in the physical, tangible realm. The Kingdom of heaven is spiritually discerned. The presence of God is all around us and within us as believers but we are free to completely ignore Him if we so choose.

How different would our church services be if Jesus were present in the flesh? Surely we would abandon all our plans and say, *"What would You like to do and say in our midst today, Lord?"* I am convinced every worship leader and Pastor would hand the reigns to Jesus immediately, should He appear in the flesh. How could we even contemplate leading God's people when God Himself is standing in our midst?

Spoiler alert: God is always in our midst - we just don't acknowledge Him and embrace His mission. All too often we end up like Jacob, as we say, *"Surely the Lord is in this place and I didn't know it!"* (Genesis 28:16)

So herein lies the great challenge for us all as we learn to live on earth as it is in heaven; as we learn to minister in and from the presence of God.

"Your kingdom come" will only be a pipedream and a prayer unless we are prepared to let go the reigns of our life, our family, our church and our community and let the King truly reign in His Kingdom.

CHAPTER FIVE
Why Did Jesus Come?

More than two thousand years ago, the Creator and Sustainer of the universe, the King of Kings, the Lord of Lords, and the second Person of the Trinity, did something that was unprecedented, astonishing, unfathomable, and almost incomprehensible: the Son of God made a decision that had an effect on all of humanity: past, present and future. He stepped out of heaven and into the womb of a Jewish adolescent to be born as a person — to become one of us. Jesus Christ, the Son of God, stepped from eternity and into time, eventually emerging as a carpenter in Nazareth. We call this the 'incarnation' and it was arguably the greatest miracle of all time. But why did Jesus come to earth?

It is likely that there are a great deal of correct responses to that question. He came to earth to die for our sins; He came to live a perfect life on our behalf; He came to usher in the Kingdom of heaven and teach us how to live as genuine people made in the image of God; He came to conquer sin, death, and Satan once and for all by rising from the dead; He came to commission us and empower us to spread the good news of God's amazing grace and salvation to the most remote parts of the world; and He came to empower us to make disciples who will make disciples who will make disciples who will make disciples!

During His time on earth, Jesus accomplished a great deal of things; but, I would like to submit to you that there is one reason that is overarching, foundational and fundamental to the reason why Jesus came into the world, and this reason is the one that influences all of the other reasons. But before I share it, I want to paint the backdrop a little further by asking another question.

What is theology? A lot of definitions have been written over the years, but in a nutshell, theology can be defined as the study of the characteristics of God. Theology is present in every sermon, hymn, worship song and on every page of the Bible. It's a fundamental component of our faith.

This investigation into the essence of God, on the other hand, is not limited to the cerebral and intellectual aspects of human consciousness. By experiencing God in all of His completeness in a manner that has an effect on our thinking, our will, and our emotions, we can only then say that we have truly studied God.

Therefore, in light of that understanding of theology, it has been said that Jesus Christ is Himself perfect theology. By that I mean anything that you think you know about God that you can't find in the person of Jesus, you have a reason to question because **Jesus came to reveal the Father.**

In order to accomplish something that had never been done before to this extent, Jesus came to earth to demonstrate to us all who God really is. That is what Jesus was meaning when He said, "*If you've seen me, you've seen the Father.*" When Jesus came to earth, He brought a revelation to all humanity which was both clear and powerful. This revelation completely surpassed any concept of God as our Father that existed in the Old Testament.

One of the most profound statements in the Bible is contained in the opening lines of the book of Hebrews, which captures the essence of our subject matter perfectly.

> *"In the past God spoke to our ancestors through the prophets at many times and in various ways, but in these last days he has spoken to us by his Son, whom he appointed heir of all things, and through whom also he made the universe. The Son is the radiance of God's glory and the exact representation of his being ..." (Hebrews 1:1-3)*

If reading that doesn't cause your heart to skip a beat – then I respectfully ask that you check you have a pulse! Jesus is the exact representation of the Father; He is God incarnate and when I right click on the word 'incarnate' my trusty thesaurus tells me that 'incarnate' means 'embodied' or 'personified' or 'alive.'

So, Jesus embodied God the Father; He personified God the Father; when Jesus came to earth, God was alive on earth through a human being. We can live ignorant of this truth, like most of the world does, or we can embrace it and understand that Jesus came to reveal God to us.

The revelation of the Father was the focus of everything Jesus did and Jesus was. Jesus said it clearly, "*I and the Father are One* … "*If you have seen me, you have seen the Father.*"

When Jesus cured Bartimaeus, who was blind, He was revealing the Father. He was doing what any father would do for their son if they had the ability to do so.

Jesus never acted in a malicious manner. His objective was to demonstrate to us what the Heavenly Father was like, and He never deviated from that purpose. God was revealed in every single action of Jesus and every single word that Jesus uttered.

This is made very plain in the fifth chapter of John. Everything that Jesus did was exactly what He observed the Father doing, and He only spoke the words that the Father had given Him to speak.

In order to fulfil the primary purpose of His coming to earth, He would not even utter a single word unless the Father had spoken it into existence first. Therefore, Jesus came to earth with this mission, this assignment, this commission, or whatever you may choose to call it. He came to unveil something that had never been revealed fully in this world before.

His purpose was to make it known to us that we have a Father Who is without flaw, Who loves us with a love that will never end, and Who has made it possible for us to be reconciled to Him forever. It truly is amazing. We are unable to comprehend it without the help of God's Spirit.

For Jesus, the revelation of the Father was His heartbeat. The Lord's personal prayer in John 17 is truly amazing. This is where Jesus stands before the Father and starts giving an account of how He has lived His life on earth. He goes through several things including, *"I made Your name manifest . . . I have declared Your word . . . I have performed Your works."* And He goes through this list of things – all of which were intended to lead people to their heavenly Father.

It was because Jesus was demonstrating to us what the Father is like that the blind were able to be healed. It was because Jesus was demonstrating to us what the Father is like, that the masses were well fed.

One day, a lady who had been caught in the act of adultery found herself at the feet of Jesus. Due to the fact that she had committed a transgression, the religious authorities gathered around her with stones, ready to kill her. These people who desired to live in accordance with the law, soon fled for their own protection when Jesus released the powerful environment of grace.

At another time, Jesus demonstrates the love that the Father has for His daughter. It is a priceless moment between a father and his daughter. Jesus is acting in the same manner as any father would if he had the opportunity to bring his daughter back to life.

He lavishes grace and forgiveness upon her, yet He does not in any way condone her wrongdoing. It was all about revealing the heart of the Father. Grace doesn't pretend there is no sin - grace enables us to live victorious over sin. So,

Jesus comes to this woman and He reveals the Father to her, thereby transforming the life of another sinner.

Maybe it has come to your attention that the only people with whom Jesus had a difficult time were the religious leaders who continued to condemn and impose restrictions on people that Jesus Himself did not impose on them. In spite of the fact that it was occasionally awkward, sinners really adored being in the presence of Jesus and would actively seek Him out.

People like Zacchaeus, who was considered to be the lowest of the low in his town. As a tax collector, he was totally despised. As a tax collector he had been stealing from his own people. He would skim off the top for his own personal gain, but Jesus never pointed that out. Can you imagine? Having a bank account full of stolen money and you want to be in the presence of God Who knows all and sees all?

Zacchaeus saw something in the person of Jesus and he was willing to risk everything he had, everything he was, for that moment of encounter.

So, Jesus looks at old Zac up the tree and says, *"I'm coming to your house. It's not good enough that you just see me from up in that tree - let's share a meal together."* I don't think any of us in this time and culture can appreciate just how amazing that was.

Or there's the prostitute who broke every rule in order to get a personal encounter with Jesus. Suddenly, she bursts into the home of a religious leader, and makes her way to where Jesus is eating. She begins to cry and she pours her tears over his feet, wiping them with her hair.

Each and every red button in those who were present that day was pushed by her actions! Without a doubt, even the disciples did not consider this was a smart idea.

However, it was necessary for them to understand that Jesus had come to reveal something different. He came to demonstrate that it is possible to exhibit mercy, grace, and kindness without condoning sin.

I believe there is still a fear in the church that if we get too loving, we will actually condone people's sin. We therefore end up focussing on the sin and become harsh and condemning. But Jesus just wasn't wired that way.

Jesus came to reveal the Father to the world. In the model prayer that Jesus taught the disciples, what is the very first word that begins the prayer? Jesus was concentrating on something that went beyond simply revealing the Father to individuals when he began his model prayer with the phrase "*Our Father.*" He was building a concept of family, of community, therefore He said when we pray we say 'our' Father, not 'my' Father.

When it comes to God's role as a Father, there are certain things that can only be learned through relationships with other people. They are not independent of each other. We individually have a relationship with God and that is precious and wonderful, but there's another whole dimension to knowing God as 'our' Father. We know God fully in community, in the family of God.

Therefore, whenever Jesus visited communities, He would walk through town and immediately attract a crowd of people around Him. They would crouch down close to Him and attempt to touch the garments He was wearing. After that, He would pause when the Holy Spirit inspired Him to do so and pray for those who were afflicted with illness or oppression.

As Jesus delivered many people from suffering, He would demonstrate the love and compassion of God, Who is a loving Father to His children.

Jesus came to reveal and release the Kingdom of heaven, which is the Kingdom in which the King is present. So, whenever that Kingdom comes into contact with this kingdom, God is always healing, delivering, restoring, forgiving, reconciling, saving and lavishing His grace, love, and mercy upon anybody who would come to Him. As a result, Jesus came to reveal the Father. I want to take you back to John chapter 20 once more.

> *"On the evening of that first day of the week, when the disciples were together, with the doors locked for fear of the Jewish leaders, Jesus came and stood among them and said, "Peace be with you!" After he said this, he showed them his hands and side. The disciples were overjoyed when they saw the Lord. Again, Jesus said, "Peace be with you! As the Father has sent me, I am sending you." And with that he breathed on them and said, "Receive the Holy Spirit."*
> *(John 20:19-22)*

Just picture yourself huddled in a room, terrified that the same people who were responsible for the death of Jesus would come looking for you. You are thinking that you might die too. While bunkered down listening to every noise outside and monitoring the windows every 30 seconds, the person whom you witnessed being executed, walks through a locked door and stands in front of you. I am not sure that would help you with your fear issues!

Perhaps that's why Jesus' first words were, *"Peace be with you."* Roughly translated it would be *"Chill guys, it's me – everything is fine!"* After releasing peace, Jesus showed them His hands and His side. Then the disciples were overjoyed when they saw it was really the Lord.

Jesus then gave them another dose of peace in verse 21 and says, *"Peace be with you! As the Father has sent me, I am sending you."* Have you ever thought about that? What did the Father send Jesus to do?

The primary reason Jesus came was to reveal the Father. So here Jesus says, *"As the Father sent me, I now send you."*

With that one statement Jesus merged His purpose with our purpose. His mission then became our mission. His reason for becoming a man, became our reason for living.

The Kingdom of God; the Kingdom of heaven, is a family run business! It has to do with family and if you miss the concept of family, you've missed the concept of God's Kingdom.

It's not a bureaucracy. It's not a religious institution. It's not an earthly government. It's not a corporation. It's none of those things. It's a family, a community.

Time after time, those in great ministries, those with great responsibilities, have learned the hard way that the church is not about building an organization. It's not about an institution. It's about being a family. The moment we miss the concept of family, we actually abandon the primary reason our Father sent Jesus and the reason Jesus sends us.

In 1654, the French philosopher and mathematician Blaise Pascal was involved in a near-fatal carriage accident, which ultimately led him to seek God's guidance. He died only 8 years later from tuberculosis yet in those final years of his life Pascal was a prolific writer. Despite the fact that many of his writings disappeared after his death, there is one quotation that has persisted and has been brought up numerous times. You might be familiar with it:

> *"There is a God-shaped vacuum in the heart of every human which cannot be satisfied by any created thing but only by God the Creator, made known through Jesus Christ."*

People are crying out to know that there is a Father in heaven Who loves them and Jesus came to reveal that Father and His love.

So in that upper room when Jesus appeared to the eleven remaining disciples He blessed them with peace and then breathed on them and said, *"Receive the Holy Spirit."*

In that amazing moment, He also said, *"My job is now your job. What the Father sent me to do, I am now sending you to do."* Which is what? To reveal the Father. That means the way we respond to a neighbour, the way we treat a business associate, the way we do church life, the way we relate to those outside the church - it's all about revealing God to people. There is an amazing prayer in Psalm 67.

> *"May God be gracious to us and bless us and make his face shine on us - so that your ways may be known on earth, your salvation among all nations." (Psalm 67:1-2)*

"God, be gracious to us and bless us." Did you know that you have an actual responsibility to pursue the blessing of God? It's not optional. Without being blessed, you will not be equipped to demonstrate what God is like.

One of the most selfish things the church has done is when, in the name of humility, we have not pursued the blessing of God. God's blessing is God's equipping.

"God be gracious to us and bless us and make his face shine on us." What is that? Well, I can tell you that neuroscientists have actually found the 'joy centre' of our brains. They've done studies and have actually written about this. They have discovered that an infant is actually trained in joy, by the joyful countenance of their caregiver – usually their mum and dad. There's something about the wrinkle in our eyes and our smile and those silly words that we say to tiny babies, you know, those words that don't exist.

It's all of that which communicates to that child, what joy is like, and it actually activates that part of their brain to experience joy. They are actually trained in joy.

When I saw that research, I could see a correlation to the lack of joy in so many Christians who have never really seen the countenance of a Father Who delights over them.

So, in Psalm 67 we have this amazing prayer asking God to fix that; to shine the light of His countenance upon us and pour out His blessing on us; to delight over us like any loving father would delight over his children; to so impact us that our own face radiates with our Father's likeness. There's something in that encounter that changes us inside.

Remember that the only time we saw the face of Moses shining is when he saw the goodness of God. God wants to change the countenance of the whole cfhurch as His goodness and love is revealed to us afresh. So, here's the prayer, *"God be gracious to us and bless us, cause Your face to shine on us."* Why? What is our motivation in asking God to shine His countenance upon us?

Verse 2 tells us: *".. so that your ways may be known on earth, your salvation among all nations."* In other words, *"Lord, if You don't do something so significant in me that it is noticeable by others, then they won't know what You are like."*

I want to give you a fresh challenge right now, that every day of your life, you be the representative of a perfect Father. I really pray that in this next season of your journey and mine, that we will boldly embrace the mission of Christ and take the baton Jesus passed to us in that upper room that day. Jesus came to reveal the Father, confident that when God is truly known on earth, everything else will fall into place. That's why He commissioned us to do the same – every day in every possible way for the rest of our lives!

Sadly, for some of us that has been very difficult because in this broken, dysfunctional world, many people have not yet had their 'joy centre' activated. They have not really experienced God's face shining on them.

Or perhaps they did once and this world and other fallen people beat it out of them and now they have many emotional and spiritual scars which reflect those beatings.

Our Father's love can heal any wound, no matter how deep or how painful. But He doesn't tend to remove the scars in this life. I used to wonder about that when for many people those scars are just a reminder of the pain they endured. But then I heard a prophetic word some time ago which really spoke to me. In this word God said, *"I'm not going to remove the scars from your life. Instead, I'm going to arrange them like a beautiful engraving on a fine piece of crystal."*

God doesn't want our scars to be a reminder of the pain and the suffering which produced them. He wants them to be a reminder of His loving grace in healing our wounds as He brought us out of that painful chapter.

Our God longs to hear us pray the prayer of Psalm 67. He is always waiting for us to open our hearts and cry out for Him to bless us and cause His face to shine upon us. Only then, can we pick up the baton Jesus passed to us. Only then, can we reveal our heavenly Father to all those around us. Only then shall His will be done on earth as it is in heaven.

CHAPTER SIX
Living in the Kingdom of Heaven

I can recall the opening words of an old hymn that was written in the 1930s by a man named Witness Lee:

> *What miracle, what mystery,*
> *that God and man should blended be.*
> *God became man to make man God,*
> *untraceable economy!*

As we continue our study into what it means to live on earth as it is in heaven, we will be continually presented with the miracle of salvation and the purposes that God has for us. The way in which God made it possible for us to be transformed into the image of His Son, our Lord Jesus Christ, and to dwell with Him for all of eternity is a marvellous act indeed. But the way in which this plan of God is carried out each day in this earthly kingdom is a mystery to us most of the time. The more I live, the more I recognise that this mystery is actually a part of God's design. This walk of faith that we have with the Lord has to have mystery.

If you understand everything that's going on in your Christian life then I think you have an inferior Christian life and you have a god who has been reduced to your own size. Mystery is just as important as understanding. What you do not know yet is just as important as what you do know.

In fact, what we don't know that still brings us to a place of trust and abandonment is really the measure of the course of faith that we've chosen to take in our life. Faith doesn't deny a problem's existence - it just denies it a place of influence. Faith refuses to allow issues to dictate our mood, our focus or our values. All of those things are inferior to the gospel of Jesus Christ.

In the last chapter, we discussed the primary purpose that Jesus came to earth, which was to reveal the Father. I would like for us to keep this in mind as we move forward and examine one of the early commissions that Jesus issued to the disciples. It is the most confronting of all and we find it in the book of Matthew.

> *"As you go, proclaim this message: 'The kingdom of heaven has come near.' Heal the sick, raise the dead, cleanse those who have leprosy, drive out demons. Freely you have received; freely give .... (v.11) Whatever town or village you enter, search there for some worthy person and stay at their house until you leave. As you enter the home, give it your greeting. If the home is deserving, let your peace rest on it; if it is not, let your peace return to you. If anyone will not welcome you or listen to your words, leave that home or town and shake the dust off your feet."* (Matthew 10: 7-8,11-14)

When Jesus urges these novice disciples to heal the sick, cleanse the lepers, drive out demons, and raise the dead, He is giving them a truly amazing assignment.

It is important to notice what Jesus does <u>not</u> say here. He doesn't tell them to pray for the sick, the lepers and the oppressed. He doesn't say to pray for the dead to be raised. He tells them to heal the sick, cast out demons and actually raise people from the dead.

I'm sure you agree that's an intimidating assignment because it's something we just can't do without the supernatural power of God. The real problem is we think the rest of the Christian life is something we can do ourselves. That's not true.

We have been called into a lifestyle that is impossible. Without the empowering presence of God, it is impossible to do what we are called and commissioned to do!

Now if that term *"the empowering presence of God"* is not immediately familiar to you, I would encourage you to read my book, Amazing Grace. The most accurate definition of the word grace is *the empowering presence of God.* Without God's empowering presence in our lives, the Kingdom of heaven is impossible to embrace, understand or even discern whilst we reside in this fallen world.

So, this command of Jesus is designed to put us into a place of utter dependency. He requires us to do something He knows we cannot do - not because He's cruel - but because when He spoke it, He made it possible.

In Luke 1:37 we have that great verse which reads, *"For nothing will be impossible with God."* That's the RSV translation, but the NIV translates the same verse as, *"No word of God will ever fail."* This is a much better translation because the word translated as 'nothing' is actually two words: the word 'no' and 'thing' and the word 'thing' here is *rhema* – the freshly spoken word of God.

So, it can actually be translated like this: *"No freshly spoken word of God will ever come to you that does not contain its own ability to perform itself."* Or in short, *'God's bidding is God's enabling.'* When the Lord gives a command, He enables what He commands. Law requires - grace enables. Always remember that!

So, the very fact that He speaks something which was completely impossible a moment earlier – now it becomes possible - because God spoke it. That's why God's commands and degrees under grace are far more difficult than the commands under the law.

Under the law we are told don't murder - under grace we are told don't even call anyone a name. Under the law we are told not to commit adultery. Under grace Jesus tells us not to even think about it.

Under grace the standard is far higher. Why? Because the enablement of grace makes it possible. God's empowering presence gives us the supernatural ability we need to reach that higher level of obedience and Kingdom living.

Therefore, when Jesus says, 'heal the sick' He is commanding us to do what is completely impossible. We may try to explain this away in order to feel more comfortable. We say that we don't heal the sick, Jesus heals the sick and calls us to be part of that.

That is probably true in one sense but the problem we have here is the text itself. Jesus didn't say *"I am going to heal the sick through you."* We'd feel better if He had said that. Or perhaps He could have said *"You just do your best and I'll back you up."* He didn't say that. He said, *"You do it."*

Jesus says that, knowing that the power to achieve what He is asking just doesn't exist in us as humans. The power to fulfill this commission must be imparted to us from God. We must receive from God before we can give to others – which is exactly what Jesus says right here.

Jesus says, *"Heal the sick, raise the dead, cleanse those who have leprosy, drive out demons. Freely you have received; freely give."* Remember Luke 1:37 that I explained earlier? *"No freshly spoken word of God will ever come to you that does not contain its own ability to perform itself."*

God spoke through Jesus and commanded the disciples to heal the sick, raise the dead, cleanse the lepers and drive out demons. With that Word comes the power to respond to that Word.

As always, Jesus is our example here. You will remember when Jesus was baptised, heaven was torn open and the Spirit of God descended and rested on Jesus and remained on Him and in Him throughout His whole ministry.

From that point on, Jesus began His ministry on earth and everything He said and did was in response to what the Father was saying and doing.

Jesus' mission on earth was only possible because He freely gave what He had freely received first. He was so conscious of the Spirit's presence that He could say, *"I only do what I see the Father doing"* and *"I only speak the words the Father gives me to speak."*

So once again we come back to the overwhelming greatest reality and priority of the Kingdom of heaven and that is the presence of God. Everywhere Jesus went, the presence of God went with Him, before Him and worked through Him. His entire mission on earth was impossible for a human being to achieve – but it became possible because Jesus was full of grace – full of the empowering presence of God.

I'm reminded of a verse tucked away in Judges 6:34 which simply says, *"Then the Spirit of the Lord came on Gideon."* When you dig down into the Hebrew behind this verse it literally says, *"The Spirit of God clothed Himself with Gideon."*

I just love that! This describes a man putting on his clothes, or a warrior putting on a suit of armour. It's like putting on a glove.

So, this verse could be translated: *"The Spirit of the Lord put Gideon on like a glove."* What a powerful picture - and what a difference it made in the life of Gideon when the Spirit of the Lord *'put him on like a glove.'* For seven straight years when the Midianites came, Gideon and the Israelites ran to their hideouts in fear. not this time. Now, empowered by the Holy Spirit, Gideon put the war trumpet to his lips and gave it a blast and everything was different. The same thing happens today when God calls His people into His service and empowers them with His Holy Spirit to do the work He has called them to do.

Let's look at verse 12 of our passage in Matthew 10. It's an obscure verse at face value, but it comes alive when you know the context. Jesus said, *"…when you go into a household, greet it. If the household is worthy, let your peace come upon it."* Just hold that thought for a moment while I take you all the way back to Noah:

> *"He (Noah) sent out from himself a dove, to see if the waters had receded from the face of the ground. But the dove found no resting place for the sole of her foot, and she returned into the ark to him, for the waters were on the face of the whole earth. So he put out his hand and took her, and drew her into the ark to himself.*
>
> *And he waited yet another seven days, and again he sent the dove out from the ark. Then the dove came to him in the evening, and behold, a freshly plucked olive leaf was in her mouth; and Noah knew that the waters had receded from the earth. So he waited yet another seven days and sent out the dove, which did not return again to him anymore."*
> *(Genesis 8:8-12)*

What is the international sign of peace? It's a dove with an olive branch in its mouth, right? Fascinating. In what form did the Holy Spirit descend and rest upon Jesus at His baptism? A dove, right? So the Old Testament story of Noah and the dove is a prophetic picture of New Testament, new covenant ministry!

Jesus said we are to go into a house and release peace there. Luke's gospel says that if there's nobody in that house worthy to receive that peace, then that dove, that peace will return to you like it did to Noah.

Now if you remember nothing else from this chapter, remember this: **You and I are ministers of a Person.** We have more than words, more than a message, more than a concept, more than a spiritual argument to give to people.

We have a Person resting upon us and residing within us Who longs to be released into the environment in which God has placed us.

What was it that was drawn from Jesus when that woman touched His garment and He felt power move from Him? What was it that was drawn from Jesus in town after town over those three and half years of intense ministry? It was the Person of the Holy Spirit – given to us without measure, without limitation to impart to any and all who receive Him. That, my friend, is the normal Christian life! That is why we are here: to advance the Kingdom of heaven, by God's grace, for God's glory and through God's Spirit.

That is what being the church is all about. That is Kingdom living. Now look at John 20:19-22. I keep coming back to this passage – and for good reason. This is after the resurrection:

> *"Then, the same day at evening, being the first day of the week, when the doors were shut where the disciples were assembled, for fear of the Jews, Jesus came and stood in the midst, and said to them, "Peace be with you."*

Remember what Jesus taught them to do when they entered a house? *'Let your peace come upon it.'* Well, this is where I think they finally understood what He was talking about.

> *"When He had said this, He showed them His hands and His side. Then the disciples were glad when they saw the Lord. So Jesus said to them again, "Peace to you! As the Father has sent Me, I also send you." And when He had said this, He breathed on them, and said to them, "Receive the Holy Spirit."*

What happened here? Jesus walked into a room full of fearful believers and released the peace of another world, another Kingdom, in the Person of the Holy Spirit. We are called to walk every day into a world full of fearful people and bring that same peace, that Person, the Holy Spirit.

Right now, we need a generation of people who can walk into a room, into a community, into a city and a nation and bring the hope, healing and reality of another world through the person of the Holy Spirit. Jesus walked into that room and said *"Peace"* and they didn't receive it at first because they were fearful.

So, Jesus said it again and His words became Spirit and He then imparted a Person to them, not a hollow platitude or a powerless blessing, but a Person. He breathed on them and said, *"Receive the Holy Spirit."*

This is so important for us to understand because living in and manifesting the reality of the Kingdom of heaven involves us learning to cooperate with the Holy Spirit and then imparting Him to others.

Do you remember in Noah's story that the dove flew around looking for a place to land? Do you understand that the Holy Spirit is always looking for a resting place in another person? He is always looking for someone to rest upon and help bring that person to their purpose in life.

I believe the Christian life is really not that complicated. It has always been about the partnership between heaven and earth so that the purposes and will of heaven would be displayed and manifested on earth. *"Your kingdom come, Your will be done on earth as it is in heaven."*

Our purpose as the church has always been to advance the Kingdom of heaven, by God's grace, for God's glory and through God's Spirit – and that Spirit has been given to every single believer - freely and without measure or limit.

Every morning as you wake, you have a choice: You can ignore, quench or grieve the Holy Spirit within you - or you can submit to Him, walk in His power and impart Him to those around you throughout that day.

It will be that choice, made each and every day by each and every one of us, which will determine if we truly are living *'on earth as it is in heaven.'*

If you want to be part of the mission of Christ to bring heaven to earth; if you want to know what kingdom living really looks like this side of the grace, then what I have shared in this chapter is not negotiable.

I shall let God have the last word, as spoken thousands of years ago through the prophet Zechariah:

> *"Not by might, nor by power, but by my Spirit,' says the Lord Almighty." (Zechariah 4:6)*

CHAPTER SEVEN
Wisdom and Power

As far as heaven is concerned, there is nothing that exists apart from the presence of God. To put it another way, you could say that abiding in Christ is a foretaste of heaven. Heaven is a complete revelation of the presence of God; it is an invitation into God's presence.

As a result, when we pray, *"Your kingdom come, Your will be done on earth as it is in heaven,"* we are actually pleading for a manifestation of the presence of God that will mark the path that history takes, mark the human heart, mark our whole way of thinking, and the values that we hold dear. At that point, the Holy Spirit Himself begins to imprint Himself on everything we do and who we really are.

In order for us to live on earth as it is in heaven, we are totally reliant on the Holy Spirit and on the presence of God. Every one of us, if we are left to our own ways, will produce a religious replica, a religious clone, which is something that only imitates what Jesus taught and did, but it is not the genuine work of Christ.

When anything is genuine, when it is born from the Spirit, it always brings complete and total liberation and freedom. The reason for this is simple: *"Where the Spirit of the Lord is, there is freedom."* (2 Corinthians 3:17)

Freedom is the manifestation of the Lordship of Jesus, which is expressed fully in the presence of God. Where the Spirit of the Lord is, we see the Lordship of Jesus in action and freedom is the evidence.

So, the Lord is always trying to bring us into freedom. Freedom is never the ability to do whatever we want. Freedom is the ability to do what is right.

That's what grace does. The Law requires, grace enables. Grace enables us to do what only Jesus can do. Grace is the empowering presence of God, which gives us the capacity to function the way Jesus functions. This relationship that we have with the Holy Spirit is absolutely central; it is life itself for us; it is the discovery and exploration of God's presence. It is true Kingdom living!

Many things are birthed in our hearts which we feel really right about, really wonderful about. However, it is not until we are immersed in the energising fire of God's presence that we come to the realisation that our conceptions of what it is to live in the Kingdom are not always in agreement with what Jesus thinks.

It is for this reason that it's so important that we are filled with the Spirit of God and that we are directed by Him at every step of the journey, just as Jesus was when He took on flesh and ministered among us all those years ago.

It is my belief that we have a deep responsibility to the world that surrounds us. We owe the world an encounter with God. We must continue to be filled with the Holy Spirit if we are to have any chance of achieving that goal.

The fact that you may pray in tongues, receive words of knowledge, or prophesy in the name of Jesus does not mean that you are filled to the brim with the Holy Spirit. You are full of the Spirit when the Spirit of God overflows from you into the lives of those around you.

Let me use an everyday illustration to explain this. When you buy a bottle of water from the shop it is legally full of water. But you can see that it's not really full at all. The only way you can be sure that it is completely full and will remain full is for you to pour more water into it until it overflows. While ever that bottle is overflowing, you know it is full to the measure.

So, the fullness of the Holy Spirit is not just a one-off experience. It's not just a theological concept. Many people are satisfied with good theology but they stop short of an actual encounter with God. We've got to take what Jesus has invited us into and follow Him into that place where the full expression of the Holy Spirit is manifest in us, every day of our lives.

Do you recall the line from Judges 6:34 that I mentioned earlier? It states that the Holy Spirit *"clothed himself with Gideon."* The image that comes to mind when one reads this is of the Holy Spirit is putting Gideon on like a glove.

When I think of a way to characterise a life that is resigned and surrendered to God the Holy Spirit, that is the finest description I could ever use.

Our connection with the Holy Spirit is also a relationship that leads to something. It establishes a seamless manifestation of who Jesus is - in and through our life. This does not involve the disintegration of our personalities; we do not stop being who we are even after this. We have not changed at all as individuals.

"All of Thee and none of me!" is a phrase that you might have said to God or heard people using. This seems to be a wonderful and introspective prayer, but this is not a request that God would ever want to hear from us. I can just hear the Lord saying, *"I had none of you before I made you and I didn't like it. That's why I made you."* So, I don't think that is ever an appropriate prayer. It's certainly evidence of humility, but what God really wants is for all of Him to fill all of us.

To put it another way, in order for us to be truly who God intends us to be, we need to be able to effortlessly manifest the presence of God, which includes His heart, His nature, His priorities, each and every day of our life.

There are many people who are capable of exhibiting the characteristics of Christ, but they have very little influence on their surroundings. This is because the empowering presence of God is not manifesting through them. So, I really believe that we owe the world a personal encounter with God, or, to put it another way, we owe the world a life that is filled with the Holy Spirit.

The very first person mentioned in the Bible who was filled with the Holy Spirit is mentioned in Exodus 31, which is a very old passage. The fullness of the Holy Spirit is described in a manner that is quite odd, but it is a really interesting description.

> *"Then the Lord said to Moses, "See, I have chosen Bezalel son of Uri, the son of Hur, of the tribe of Judah, and I have filled him with the Spirit of God, with wisdom, with understanding, with knowledge and with all kinds of skills - to make artistic designs for work in gold, silver and bronze, to cut and set stones, to work in wood, and to engage in all kinds of crafts." (Exodus 31:1-5)*

It is amazing to me that the first person in the Bible to be filled with the Spirit was for the purpose of gaining the understanding necessary to be brilliant and creative in their work.

At this point, let us jump ahead in time to the New Testament. Here we see people touching the clothes that Jesus is wearing, and they are healed. Jesus then announces, "... *Greater works than these shall you do,*"

That's what happened when the Apostle Paul was ministering too. They would collect aprons and sweatbands from his body and take them some distance to lay them on a demonized or sick person. The demons would cry out and leave or the disease would be healed. Really? What is the point here?

Obviously, sweatbands and aprons were not considered to be preaching garb; they were not considered to be the three-piece suit of their time. However, Paul was so filled with the Spirit of God that people could remove the sweatband from his head after he had spent the entire day making tents - the sweat from his brow while he was working - and take it to a person who was demonised, and they would be set free, just like the people who touched the garment that Jesus was wearing.

However, this is pushed to a whole other level here. Well, that's exactly what the Lord intends to do in our generation is to take what He did, and take it to another level.

So, in the Old Testament, the first person filled with the Spirit of God was a person filled for the purpose of work. Work should be something that the church understands because the Jewish community grew up with this understanding that their work is actually worship.

As the church today, we look forward to coming together on Sunday, or in other special events. These are highlights for us in our walk with the Lord. But the impact that we have, is not just through the witnessing that we do at work and in the world. It is through the excellence, the creativity, the uniqueness of our labour throughout our life; our devotion to working well and working hard.

But it's not just the quality of the work. It's the fact that what we do, from our heart we do as unto the Lord (See Colossians 3:23). So, this first person filled with the Holy Spirit we see in the Old Testament, was filled for the purpose of labour.

Let's look again at the first part of verse 3 in Exodus 31.

The Lord says, *"I have filled him with the Spirit of God, (and) with wisdom ..."*

I want to highlight the word *wisdom,* because everything that follows (which you can read in the book of Proverbs) is a manifestation of wisdom.

Wisdom was there on the day of creation, assisting in the creative expression of the earth. It's in Proverbs chapter eight. Wisdom is measurable in creativity, integrity and excellence. You can see the silver thread of creativity, integrity and excellence all through the book of Proverbs revealing the importance of wisdom.

This is something that I am bringing up for a reason, and that is because the world is currently in desperate need of answers to problems that we just do not have. Undoubtedly, I am a firm believer in the courageous proclamation of the gospel. I am a firm believer in the need of communicating our faith to others and praying for them both in public and in private settings. All of that is something that I believe in.

In the end, however, we need to be a people who are able to come to the table with answers, solutions, and something that is genuinely beneficial to the people, not just to those of us who are members of the church.

To be salt and light in the world is a calling that has been given to the church, and this does not simply mean proclaiming the name of Jesus and inviting people to follow Him. It also implies that the church is the channel via which the omnipotent wisdom of God Himself is communicated to the whole world and, according to Paul, even to celestial beings (Ephesians 3:10).

When the manifest presence of God fills us and overflows into the environment around us, everyone should benefit: business leaders, community leaders and political leaders can all come to a place of greater effectiveness if the people of God can hear from the Lord and function in this gift called wisdom.

I personally think that divine wisdom is one of the most important missing elements in our culture today. Wisdom is divine reasoning. Having wisdom means having the ability to understand things from the God's perspective.

In addition, it is not enough to simply have effective answers for issues. It is not as simple as that. Having the ability to see beneath the surface and get to the core of a situation, a group of people, or a crisis is what it means to exercise wisdom. Just by looking at a wall that has been plastered, I can see nothing but painted plaster.

However, if I am able to see through that plaster, I will be able to recognise the studs, noggins, nails, and even pencil marks that were left behind by the person who constructed the wall. Wisdom is the ability to see into the inner workings of anything that will not be immediately apparent. In other words, wisdom is prophetic in its nature as it looks into the heart of something. That's why wisdom is always able to bring long-term solutions to problems.

Wisdom is what the world around us is genuinely yearning for, regardless of whether they are aware of it or not, and the church is the conduit through which the manifold wisdom of God can flow into the world. That's and me! It is for this reason that I would like to suggest that the first manifestation of the fullness of the Holy Spirit in the Bible is in wisdom. Ok, let's jump over into the New Testament now – the book of Acts.

> *"When the day of Pentecost came, they were all together in one place. Suddenly a sound like the blowing of a violent wind came from heaven and filled the whole house where they were sitting. They saw what seemed to be tongues of fire that separated and came to rest on each of them. All of them were filled with the Holy Spirit and began to speak in other tongues as the Spirit enabled them.*

> *Now there were staying in Jerusalem God-fearing Jews from every nation under heaven. When they heard this sound, a crowd came together in bewilderment, because each one heard their own language being spoken. Utterly amazed, they asked: "Aren't all these who are speaking Galileans?*
>
> *Then how is it that each of us hears them in our native language? Parthians, Medes and Elamites; residents of Mesopotamia, Judea and Cappadocia, Pontus and Asia, Phrygia and Pamphylia, Egypt and the parts of Libya near Cyrene; visitors from Rome (both Jews and converts to Judaism); Cretans and Arabs - we hear them declaring the wonders of God in our own tongues!"*
>
> *Amazed and perplexed, they asked one another, "What does this mean?" Some, however, made fun of them and said, "They have had too much wine." (Acts 2:1-13)*

Confused, amazed, marvelled, bewildered, perplexed, mocking. Sounds like a revival to me! Every time throughout history when God shows up in a mighty way, we see all those responses.

The manifestation of the fullness of the Holy Spirit in Acts chapter two is not just for the ability to speak in tongues; it is not just for the ability to be a witness in the sense of being brave for Christ; it is all of those things and more.

The bottom line is that the reason for the outpouring of the Holy Spirit in Acts chapter two is for *power*.

This is exactly what Jesus had predicted when He instructed the disciples that they should not leave Jerusalem but rather wait for the gift that the Father had given.

> *" ... you will receive power when the Holy Spirit comes on you; and you will be my witnesses in Jerusalem, and in all Judea and Samaria, and to the ends of the earth." (Acts 1:8)*

Consequently, if we want to consider the Old Testament interpretation of being full of the spirit as being for wisdom, then the New Testament interpretation ought to be for power. That said, I would want to make the suggestion that whenever God reveals anything new, He never undoes what He has revealed in the past.

For instance, when Jesus says, "*I no longer call you servants, I now call you friends ...*" He is revealing this tremendous new intimacy that He is bringing us into, but He is not doing away with the concept of servanthood. Instead, He established friendship on the foundation of servanthood.

That's why you can have somebody as intimate as Paul is with God, calling himself a bondservant of the Lord. Servanthood never disappeared, it just became the foundation for something more that God is building and revealing. Therefore, the goal of the fullness of the Spirit being described in the Old Testament was to bring forth wisdom. That foundation was strengthened by the addition of power, which God then introduced in the New Testament.

I've heard it expressed that wisdom is the setting on the ring, and power is the diamond. This is a helpful representation of this concept. In the event that we are successful in bringing about a generation that is capable of functioning in both wisdom and power, then the church will finally bring the transformation that is required in our broken and needy world. Changes in sickness, war, famine, and every other area of need that is all around us every day; and changes in our entire culture.

But despite the fact that there are a lot of really lovely people in the world who are extremely kind of very service-oriented and even quite wise, they do not have the power to change the things that need to be changed.

In the Bible, the concept of 'power' is quite straightforward. The literal translation of *power* is '*the ability to do.*'

Jesus instructed His disciples to remain in Jerusalem and not to leave, and not to even attempt to fulfil their calling in order to carry on His mission. They were required to wait for power, for the ability to do what they were unable to do, and that power arrived when they were filled with the Holy Spirit.

Only after that, would they be able to fully embrace what we now call the great commission and genuinely make a difference in the world, just like Jesus did while He was ministering in their midst.

In the last chapter, I talked about the totally impossible commission that Jesus gave to the disciples in Matthew 10. He told them to heal the sick, cleanse the lepers, cast out demons and raise the dead. It was completely impossible for any of those disciples to do any of those things.

This was something that Jesus had commissioned them to accomplish, but they lacked the power to do so. For some of them, that power came upon them in the upper room when Jesus breathed on them and said, "*Receive the Holy Spirit.*" For many others, it came upon them on the day of Pentecost when the Holy Spirit was poured out on many people.

Perhaps we could put it this way: *Power is what ignites the fires of revival, but wisdom is what keeps them burning.* Wisdom establishes a framework within which the movement of God can continue.

As a generation, you and I have been called to be a people who are filled with the Spirit; who know what it is to host the Spirit of God; to truly yield to this wonderful Person; to fellowship with Him; to walk with Him; talk with Him and to move to His most subtle impressions.

Wisdom is what gives longevity to anything that God is doing on earth, and we have been called to be a people who are filled with the Spirit. The Lord is searching not merely for a display of His might, He wants to witness His might in action over the long haul.

There have been many mighty moves of God and many amazing manifestations of His power throughout my life, but very few of them have produced fruit over the long haul. This is due to the fact that the servants who were a part of those outpourings lacked the wisdom of God to channel that power into long-term ministry and complete community transformation.

That is the plan that God has had from the very beginning. This is what it looks like to advance the kingdom of heaven, by God's grace, for God's glory, in the power of God's Spirit. Revival is what we need to be praying for each and every day, and this is how it will happen.

When I look at the Church across the world today, I see some hot spots where the power of God is simply awesome and lots of people are being impacted in mighty ways. But I know from experience that most of those hot spots will burn out or grow cold in the days to come because those leaders lack the wisdom of God to keep the fires burning.

I also see many incredibly wise teachers, preachers and Bible Scholars – people who can articulate the truth better than anyone and who wear the wisdom of God like a cloak. But their ministry lacks the power to transform people and whole communities and address the deepest needs our world faces today. What we should be praying for every day is a manifestation of the wisdom and power of God across the whole church as we are filled to the measure of the fullness of God. Then, and only then, will we begin to live on earth as it is in heaven.

CHAPTER EIGHT
Embracing a Kingdom Worldview

A remarkable exchange takes place between Jesus and His first disciples in the eighth chapter of Mark's gospel. It is actually a valuable lesson about the importance of having a renewed mind. As a matter of fact, I believe the gospel of Mark illustrates the renewed mind better than any part of the Bible. A renewed mind is necessary for the practice of our faith. Every single day of our lives in this earthly kingdom, the Holy Spirit is working on us to renew our minds. This is because it is God's desire to eclipse this kingdom with the Kingdom of heaven, and our renewed minds are an essential component of that process.

> *"Therefore, I urge you, brothers and sisters, in view of God's mercy, to offer your bodies as a living sacrifice, holy and pleasing to God - this is your true and proper worship. Do not conform to the pattern of this world but be transformed by the renewing of your mind. Then you will be able to test and approve what God's will is - his good, pleasing and perfect will." (Romans 12:1-2)*

Paul urges us, through the Holy Spirit, to not conform to this world but rather undergo a transformation that is brought about by the complete renewal of our minds. Why? So we might test and approve the will of God. What is the will of God? Simply put: heaven on earth is the will of God. That's why Jesus told us to pray, *"Your will be done, on earth, as it is in heaven."* So, what does a renewed mind do? It proves the will of God as it unfolds through His Kingdom impacting the kingdom of this world.

The mind which has not been renewed can only view this earthly kingdom and make decisions based on an earthly worldview.

By contrast, the renewed mind is able to embrace the Kingdom of heaven, and this is supposed to transform our entire way of thinking so that we can see God at work in His kingdom as it advances and eclipses this earthly kingdom. As a result, we are able to observe that what is true in heaven is gradually becoming true on earth.

The renewed mind is able to see what is real in the Kingdom of heaven, which in turn produces faith to believe that the reality of heaven can become a reality in this world. In heaven, there is no cancer, no death, no oppression, no demons, no doubt, no fear, and no loneliness. Jesus called us to pray for and believe that God's will can and should prevail *on earth as it is in heaven.* The renewed mind produces a Kingdom worldview.

However, the renewed mind is not the source of our faith. Faith doesn't come from the mind - it comes from the heart. Faith is not the product of striving – it's the result of surrender and surrender is always a heart issue. But the renewed mind creates the context for faith to flow – just like the banks of a river.

So, the Lord is always wanting to renew our mind. Let's now look at this very interesting conversation between Jesus and His disciples.

> *"And He left them, and getting into the boat again, departed to the other side. Now the disciples had forgotten to take bread, and they did not have more than one loaf with them in the boat. Then He charged them, saying, "Take heed, beware of the leaven of the Pharisees and the leaven of Herod."*
> *And they reasoned among themselves, saying, "It is because we have no bread." But Jesus, being aware of it, said to them, "Why do you reason because you have no bread? Do you not yet perceive nor understand? Is your heart still hardened? Having eyes, do you not see? And having ears, do you not hear?*

> *And do you not remember? When I broke the five loaves for the five thousand, how many baskets full of fragments did you take up?" They said to Him, "Twelve." "Also, when I broke the seven for the four thousand, how many large baskets full of fragments did you take up?" And they said, "Seven." So, He said to them, "How is it you do not understand?" (Mark 8:13-21)*

I believe that this particular passage of the Bible is the one that we ought to read over and over again, particularly in light of the current circumstances in which we find ourselves in this broken, dysfunctional world. I want to focus on verse 17.

> *"Jesus, being aware of it, said to them, "Why do you reason because you have no bread? Do you not yet perceive nor understand? Is your heart still hardened?" (Mark 8:17)*

Any thought process that begins with what we don't have, will have to be repented of later, because you cannot build anything substantial on that negative thought. It makes a poor foundation for human reasoning. So, Jesus gives them this very important instruction. He warns them about leaven: the leaven of Herod, and the leaven of the Pharisees. There is a third kind of leaven in the Bible, it's in Matthew 13, it is the leaven of the Kingdom. Leaven is yeast which you work into dough and that causes it to rise before you cook it and the end result will be delicious bread.

Jesus warns us about two different kinds of leaven. In our context, leaven is our worldview - our way of thinking and interpreting the world. Jesus warns against the religious worldview of the Pharisees and the political worldview of Herod. The leaven of the Pharisees is dangerous because it has God at the centre of everything, but the God in religion is impersonal, powerless, figurative and not relational. That is what produces the religious worldview.

Now the Kingdom worldview is the opposite of both of those. God is *really* at the centre of everything, and defines everything by His own person, His own presence. That is, everything is defined by the person of the Lord Jesus Christ: every value, every principle, every thought. In Him we live and move and have our being.

This Kingdom worldview is radically different to the religious and political worldviews. Jesus warns us about these value systems that can and will lead us away from the reality of the Kingdom of heaven, which is the greatest reality of all and the only reality which is eternal. The Apostle Paul told us what you can't see is eternal and what you can see is temporal.

> *"For the kingdom of God is not eating and drinking, but righteousness and peace and joy in the Holy Spirit."*
> *(Romans 14:17)*

Jesus is constantly wanting to instil in us the understanding of who we are and what we are here to do. Jesus is always trying to build in us a deep awareness of our identity and purpose, so that we can effectively use His name and authority to accomplish His purposes. It's not about *our* little kingdoms or *our* fame or success or any of those things. It's not about the fulfilment of *our* dreams. Fulfilling our dreams must always be the by-product of fulfilling His. If you ever think God is not listening to your prayers, maybe you could talk to Him about something He likes to talk about! Talk to God about what He thinks is important.

Therefore, the political spirit and the religious spirit which Jesus discusses in Mark 8, have something in common. If you study the Gospels, you'll see this repeated over and over again. Both of them are heavily influenced by the fear of man. Have you noticed how the Pharisees wouldn't answer a question for fear the crowd would turn on them?

Whereas the political system refused to make a decision. Pilate ended up washing his hands of this whole Jesus situation thereby opening the door for Him to be crucified because of the political environment at the time. Pilate feared the crowd would tell Caesar and turn on him. The motivation for so many decisions in both the religious and the political worldview is the fear of man. But what's really amazing is they all think this is wisdom! Fear masquerades as wisdom, it doesn't matter what it is, fear will always attract whatever information is needed to legitimize its existence. Fear reinforces itself.

I want to make a side comment here. Each of us have strengths, but those strengths have the potential to become weaknesses. Although the Apostle Peter was known for his fearlessness, it did not always work out so well for him, did it? In contrast, after it was brought under the authority of Jesus, it functioned really well. Therefore, the fear of man frequently starts with a tender heart that is filled with compassion and genuine concern for others. Whereas on the other hand, Satan is always hard at work manipulating everything so that we are actually governed by the gift, rather than us managing the gift for the benefit of the Kingdom of heaven.

Let's go back to end of the story now in Mark 8. Jesus talks to these guys and first, He says:

> *"When I broke the five loaves for the five thousand, how many baskets full of fragments did you take up?" They said to Him, "Twelve." "Also, when I broke the seven for the four thousand, how many large baskets full of fragments did you take up?" And they said, "Seven." (Mark 8:19-20)*

Did you notice that when Jesus fed the most people, He started with the least amount of food, and He had the most left over? In the Kingdom of heaven, starting with more is not an advantage.

Starting with more may be the Wall Street perspective – that's this earthly kingdom's worldview, but that's not the Kingdom of God, the Kingdom of heaven. You were chosen, not for your strengths, but for your weaknesses.

> *"Why do you reason because you have no bread? Do you not yet perceive nor understand? Is your heart still hardened?" (Mark 8:17)*

Because of our conversion, we now have the ability to see into God's Kingdom. We can see heaven! In the third chapter of John, Jesus explains to Nicodemus that unless we are born again, we will not be able to embrace the reality of the kingdom of heaven. One of the implications of our conversion is that it enables us to perceive everything through the lens of a Kingdom worldview.

Now, in this text, Jesus confronts the disciples and asks them why they are unable to perceive the reality that is right in front of them. He never does that out of shame. He will never rub our nose in our shortcomings. It's never to make us feel hopeless. It's always an invitation to maturity. It's always an invitation to grow. Jesus is just pointing out some of the weaknesses in the disciples' perception.

If you read the previous verses in chapter Mark chapter 8 you will see that these disciples were only just used by God to multiply food a second time for the 4,000. So, they go from yet another miracle of multiplying food to this boat and they're afraid of not having enough food for lunch?! You can see now why Jesus asked them, *"Why do you reason because you have no bread?"* In other words, *"Why did you start your thinking with what you don't have?"*

Now it is important that we take note of the fact that this was not the first day on the job for these disciples. Jesus didn't ask a question like this when they had no experience whatsoever of the supernatural work of God.

These disciples had some history, some very recent history, in fact, of God's provision and power and the reality of the Kingdom of heaven invading the kingdom of this world. So, to put it bluntly, they should have known better than to worry about having enough for lunch – given what they had seen, experienced and been part of during this amazing ministry journey with Jesus!

Under no circumstances would Jesus have posed such a question to them when they were just beginning their journey as disciples, nor would He have anticipated that they would have reached that level of comprehension. They needed to have encountered the God of the impossible, the God of unlimited supply, the God who invades this broken world and meets people's needs, physically and spiritually. But now that they have experienced multiplying food twice, it should have shifted their perspective. Such experiences in the Kingdom of heaven are supposed to change the way we deal with all the situations of our life.

Let me put it really clearly: Once you've witnessed the supernatural supply of God, you no longer have the right to start any thought process with what you don't have!

Encountering the supernatural should produce a shift in our worldview; it should change the whole way we think, reason and understand the world. Any thought process that starts with what you don't have will have to be repented of later because anything you build on that thought is built on sand; it's built on a weak foundation.

People around you might applaud you and call it common sense – but common to what world? What kingdom is it common to? *"Why do you reason that you have no bread? Don't you understand? Can you not perceive?"* Then Jesus goes on and He asks three questions. *"Having eyes, do you not see? And having ears, do you not hear? And do you not remember?"*

Now with the first two, most of us would attribute to somebody who has a particular gift. I have met many people who have the ability to see into God's Kingdom and God's heart more than most and others who seem to hear from God all the time in very specific ways.

These are undoubtedly gifts which God has given the church through some people and not through others and you may not have such a gift in this particular season of your life ... but you can always remember.

In Psalm 119:111 we read, *"The testimony of the Lord is your inheritance forever."* Say that out loud: *"The testimony of the Lord is your inheritance forever."* Now make it personal. *"The testimony of the LORD is my inheritance forever."*

Now note that this verse does not say your testimony is your inheritance forever. It says the testimony of the Lord, which then opens it up to everything God has ever done across all time, in His love relationship with His people; in all His activities with all His people. That then means that when the water came out of the rock, for Israel, that's *your* story. That's *my* story – that's part of *our* inheritance.

Now at times people don't enjoy their inheritance. They don't use their inheritance, they leave it where it is, you know, they may inherit a home but they never live there. Well sadly, a lot of us who have this great inheritance in God, never embrace or enjoy what is ours. But these are all *our* stories.

In Luke 7 we read where Jesus came upon a funeral procession of a dead child and the mother who was also a widow was weeping. The Father's heart in Jesus was deeply moved with compassion and He touched the coffin and told the young boy to get up – and he did. Guess what? That's *your* story! Why? Why is this important?

Because prayerfully meditating on the testimony of the Lord equips you with an ability to see and hear God better in your journey.

Jesus has His disciples cornered, they're on a boat and they can't go anywhere. He says, *"Why do you reason because you have no bread? Do you not yet perceive nor understand? Is your heart still hardened? Having eyes can't you see? Having ears Can you hear? Can you at least remember?"*

If you are anything like me, then there are times when you can't really see what God is doing and often those times coincide with spiritual deafness. We pray and pray but get nothing. We know that God is always at work and always speaking but we just can't hear Him or see what He is doing.

We might make ourselves feel better by assuming that only those with special gifts can see and hear God. That's not true, but we know there are gifts associated with those first two questions from Jesus. But then He leaves us without excuse as He hits us with this third question, *"Do you not remember?"* The first two questions may be attributed to gifts but this third one is attributed to willingness and it applies to every one of us, every day of our lives. *"Do you not remember?"*

I know from personal experience that at those times when I feel dry and can't seem to see or hear God – I try to remember God's faithfulness, God's provision and God's miraculous intervention. I have been part of some pretty amazing ministry times where God has healed people from all manner of ailments, injuries, sickness and even genetic malformations.

So, I have my own history with God which is really 'His Story' as I have experienced it. Added to that I have a Bible which is full of amazing stories of God's grace, mercy, power, blessing and abundant provision for His people.

I can remember and so can you. I can indeed say, *"The testimony of the LORD is my inheritance forever,"* and so can you. It is my prayer that everybody reading this book will literally be a magnet for hope and that our faith, our testimonies and all the things that reinforce why we are here, why we are alive, would not be void of the supernatural interventions of God.

I pray that God will open eyes and ears every day to see the wonders of His Kingdom as it invades our lives, our church and our world.

I also pray that the Holy Spirit will cause us to remember the testimony of the Lord. For He Who promised is faithful and He will do it - in His time and in His way – but He will always do it. We have proof of that on every page of the Bible and in every chapter of our lives as we remember the faithfulness, provision and supernatural intervention of God throughout our earthly journey with Him.

May we hear those challenging words from Jesus afresh today, *"Having eyes, do you not see? And having ears, do you not hear? And do you not remember?"*

CHAPTER NINE
The Mystery of the Kingdom

There are actually 60 parables of Jesus in the Bible. Some of them are repeated in the Gospels and so the number of individual parables is 43. Some of those parables are specifically about the Kingdom of heaven and they are grouped together in Matthew 13 and Mark 4.

The first of those parables is the parable of the Sower. This is one of the most well-known of Jesus' parables and arguably the most important. That's not my opinion, Jesus Himself said so. In the Gospel of Mark we read, *"Do you not understand this parable? How will you understand all the parables?"* (Mark 4:13).

Jesus is suggesting that the parable of the Sower is the key to unlocking all the other parables and so I want us to look at this parable here because it contains some foundational truths for Kingdom living.

> *"And the disciples came and said to (Jesus), "Why do You speak to them in parables?" He answered and said, "Because it has been given to you to know the mysteries of the kingdom of heaven, but to them it has not been given."*
> *(Matthew 13:10-11)*

In this parable we have the illustration of the nature and the purpose of the Word of God. Now I really value the voice of God, more than I can explain, but my value for the voice of God has to be represented in my value for Scripture. If I value the voice of God above Scripture, then I am open to deception. The voice of God will never contradict Scripture.

In a day when it's so easy to have the Bible in print and on our devices and in many different translations - there's absolutely no excuse for Biblical illiteracy.

We all should give ourselves to the study of Scripture, but it is the voice of God through the Holy Spirit that brings the Word of God to life for us and in us. Without the voice of God, through the Holy Spirit, the Bible is just a dusty old book with no power to change us or the world.

So, in this parable Jesus says that if we want to understand all His other parables, we first need to understand this one. Now the Word of God is the seed and the human heart is the soil. Tender soil receives the Word and the life of God brings about the change God intends. Or in Paul' words:

> *"For this reason we also thank God without ceasing, because when you received the word of God which you heard from us, you welcomed it not as the word of men, but as it is in truth, the word of God, which also effectively works in you who believe."* (1 Thessalonians 2:13)

In the original Greek language behind this verse, the word of God actually represents or contains the energy of God. So, when God speaks to us, it comes in seed form and the energy of God brings the fruitfulness that He intended. The heart is the soil and the seed is the Word of God.

Most people read the parable of the Sower in Matthew 13. But I want us to look at Mark's version in his gospel. But before I do that, I want to take you to a couple of other verses first – in Hebrews and James.

I want to set the stage here before looking at the main text. I am sure you have heard this before but it's good to be reminded. One of my favourite sayings from the Reformer, Martin Luther is, *"We need to hear the gospel every day, because we forget it every day."*

Hearing the gospel is what recalibrates the compass of our heart, so we know exactly where 'true north' is; so we know what is important in God's eyes.

All of that is defined by hearing the purity, the simplicity, and the power of the gospel every day!

> *" ... by this time you ought to be teachers, you need someone to teach you the elementary truths of God's word all over again. You need milk, not solid food! Anyone who lives on milk, being still an infant, is not acquainted with the teaching about righteousness. But solid food is for the mature, who by constant use have trained themselves to distinguish good from evil." (Hebrews 5:12-14)*

The Word of God comes to us in several forms, or the Word has several different roles or assignments, if you like. One is the 'milk' of the Word. The milk of the Word is that which comforts and encourages. The 'meat' of the Word is identified here as the Word of righteousness. The meat of the Word is that which provokes and brings about change and growth.

It's the transformational Word of God, provoking us to recognize what God is telling us needs to happen and it brings us into a place where we yield to the purposes of God. So, there's the milk – which comforts and encourages. Then there's the meat which confronts, exhorts and provokes us to change.

But the third role of the Word is in the area of promise. There are actually over 7,700 separate promises of God in the Scriptures. Word of God deposits promise in us and defines our hope-filled future and what is possible for us when we live on earth as it is in heaven.

Now the Word of God may come in many forms, but these are three that we need to understand. There is the comfort of the Word - the milk - that which soothes, gives peace and encourages us; then there's the Word of righteousness - that which exposes what's in us that needs to change and gives us the motivation to pursue that transformation.

Then there's the third form in which the Word of God brings the promise for a hopeful future. Hebrews 5:14 then says that solid food belongs to those who are mature. That is those who by constant use have their senses trained to discern both good and evil. This is a really great verse and it so violates Western culture. Other translations say these mature people have 'trained their senses' to discern between good and evil.

This verse basically says that your maturity as a believer is going to be measured by your ability to train your own senses to recognize a difference between good and evil. Our senses - sight, hearing, smell, taste, touch – all can be trained. Everything about you was perfectly designed to recognize and enjoy close fellowship with God.

Everything about you, that includes every sense; every one of your personality traits; everything in you that God put in you was designed so that you can recognize Him and commune with Him and enjoy fellowship with Him and minister with Him. Let's look at one more verse which we find in James chapter one.

> "Therefore put away all filthiness and rank growth of wickedness and receive with meekness the implanted word, which is able to save your souls." (James 1:21)

Receive with meekness the implanted word. This is a wonderful picture that James is giving us here. The New American Standard Bible puts it this way, "*In humility (that's a condition of heart), receive the word implanted, which is able to save your soul.*" The ability is in the Word of God.

The life is in the Word, not the soil. The soil creates the condition, the atmosphere, but the energy of God is in the seed. The energy of God takes root in a person to illustrate who God is - it's always to reveal Him. Now let's go to Mark's gospel and look at this wonderful parable.

> *"Listen! Behold, a Sower went out to sow. And it happened, as he sowed, that some seed fell by the wayside; and the birds of the air came and devoured it. Some fell on stony ground, where it did not have much earth; and immediately it sprang up because it had no depth of earth. But when the sun was up it was scorched, and because it had no root it withered away. And some seed fell among thorns; and the thorns grew up and choked it, and it yielded no crop. But other seed fell on good ground and yielded a crop that sprang up, increased and produced: some thirtyfold, some sixty, and some a hundred. And He said to them, "He who has ears to hear, let him hear!" But when He was alone, those around Him with the twelve asked Him about the parable. And He said to them, "To you it has been given to know the mystery of the kingdom of heaven ..." (Mark 4:1-11a)*

Say this out loud: **To me it has been given to know the mystery of the kingdom of heaven.** God has already given us a key to perceive unseen realities. Let's skip down to verse 13.

> *"Then Jesus said to them, "Don't you understand this parable? How then will you understand any parable? The farmer sows the word. Some people are like seed along the path, where the word is sown. As soon as they hear it, Satan comes and takes away the word that was sown in them. Others, like seed sown on rocky places, hear the word and at once receive it with joy. But since they have no root, they last only a short time. When trouble or persecution comes because of the word, they quickly fall away. Still others, like seed sown among thorns, hear the word; but the worries of this life, the deceitfulness of wealth and the desires for other things come in and choke the word, making it unfruitful." (Mark 4:13-19)*

Then Jesus talks about the seed that's planted in good soil.

The seed thrown on the wayside - this should be an obvious picture. It's on trampled ground; it's a hardened surface; it does not receive the seed; that seeds sits there on the surface so it's easy for the birds of the air to come and steal that seed. When there's hardness of heart in us, we may hear all the right things, but there's no breaking of the soil to receive that seed. So, it's very easy for the enemy to snatch it away.

The second image is of rocky soil. Rocky soil should also be fairly easy to understand. The rocks in our soil, in our heart, are things like regret, resentment, bitterness and all the issues of heart that just never get dealt with season after season. Those things then become part of our life and our personality and form barriers to the life-giving Seed of the Word of God. We may hear the Word, but there is no depth in us to receive what God is saying because the rocks are blocking the seed from going deep.

Then there is the one which I want to talk to you about here, it's in verse 18 and that's when the seed is sown among thorns. This represents those of us who hear the Word, but then the cares of this world, the deceitfulness of riches and the desires for other things, enter in and choke the Word.

Please understand this: you and I, with our thoughts, attitudes and appetites, have the capacity to put a stranglehold on the promise that God has given us in Christ.

Jesus is talking here about us giving thorns an opportunity to grow. We all know from our own lawns and gardens that thorns and weeds grow bigger, faster and stronger than the good plants we want to grow.

It's a weird thing – it's probably another result of the fall – I doubt there were any weeds or thorns in the Garden of Eden – but we don't know. In this parable, the meaning is very clear. Here Jesus is saying that the thorns of the world choke the Word of the Lord if we let them.

That means the promise on your life can actually be choked or strangled by the deceitfulness of riches, the cares of this world, and the desire for other things.

Let's break down those three things. The phrase *'cares of this world'* actually comes from two words in the Greek. The first means *divided* and the second is *mind*. So, the thorn to avoid here is a divided mind. A lot of people experience stress, anxiety and confusion because their mind is divided. They just have too many options; they have Jesus and all these other options. That creates a conflict for them which ultimately chokes the good seed – the clear, unambiguous Word of God.

Many years ago, I remember reading a story about this guy who was a great athlete and loved competition. He loved sports of all kinds. He ended up in a horrible accident and lost an arm. He spent a lot of time after that trying to find some kind of a sport that he could be involved in with only one arm. He ended up choosing the sport of handball.

Now if you have ever played proper handball, you will know it can be quite painful. It's a very intense and competitive sport. Well, this one-armed man became quite good over time and was crowned the club champion and ended up competing at a state level where he finally won the championship!

Following his final match, a newspaper reporter wanted to interview him. His first question was this: *"How is it that a man with only one hand can defeat all your opponents who can play with two hands?"* He said, *"That's easy: options."* The reporter asked him to explain what he meant by 'options.' He said, *"Well, it's like this, when the ball comes off the wall, my opponent has to decide what hand he's going to use, whereas I only have one option. My decision was made for me when I lost my arm – so I only have one option and that means it's always easier for me to win."*

I believe many of us allow ourselves too many options and at that point we are inviting confusion into our lives. When you invite confusion, you open the door to anxiety, worry, and unnecessary stress. Just like that handball champion, we will always have the upper hand, when we only have one option. Our only option should be, *"I'm hungry for the will of God. I don't care what it tastes like in the moment. It's what I'm hungry for. It's what I want."*

In John 4:34 Jesus said, *"My food is to do the will of Him who sent me and to finish His work."* Now I am sure you know that sometimes the will of God brings a sour or bitter taste to the mouth – but it's always pleasant to the stomach. The will of man is often sweet to the taste - but it turns sour in the stomach. There's something about the will of God that nourishes and strengthens us deep down – even if it's not pleasant at the time. The 'cares of this world,' which equates to a divided mind, will always lead to anxiety and worry.

Think about it this way: every moment that you and I spend in worry and anxiety, equates to us feeding the thorns and weeds which strangle that promise over our lives. Every second I spend worrying, I'm actually feeding the beast that is working to put a stranglehold over the promises of God for my life. The devil cannot read our thoughts but he can certainly read the thoughts he puts into our minds! He can tell before we can, when one of his suggestions (the Bible calls them fiery darts) has made it past our shield of faith, because it affects our whole demeanour. Such is the result of the thorn of the cares of this world - the divided mind.

The second thorn is the deceitfulness of riches. Notice it doesn't say riches. It says there's a deceitfulness that can come with riches if we're not alert. Riches can include money, resources, all our possessions, but in also includes our position, title, accomplishments and the abundance that we have in our life.

The deceitfulness that comes with riches is when we think we have power because of our riches. This affects us all because on a grand scale, we are all rich and with riches there is often an illusion of power and personal significance.

That increases with more possessions or more money. However, neither riches nor poverty create our heart attitude – but they can reveal our heart. Let me stress that again: neither riches nor poverty create the attitude of our heart, but they most certainly can reveal it.

People may ask, 'how much is too much money?' Well, I guess that will depend on your heart. It is whatever amount causes you to not trust anymore. For one person, having $5,000 in the bank may cause them to no longer trust God because they only trust Him when they're in constant need and constant prayer and constant dependency. As soon as they get a little nest-egg it can so easily replace trust.

How much is too much? It is whatever amount replaces trust. For another person, it could be a million dollars - because their default level of trust is high.

True spirituality is always birthed in a relationship of trust. It's not what I own or don't own. So much wealth is used to create image and image is just the soul-less attempt to create identity. It's the counterfeit role of creating identity in the life of a believer.

My identity is not in what I own. It's not in my title. It's not even in how God uses me. It's none of those things. I am a child of God who was adopted by the most gracious Father and my identity is in the One Who called me to Himself. That's it completely. Everything else is a bonus. Everything else is extra. Everything else is secondary in importance and will never define who I really am. But the deceitfulness of riches will always create a sense of entitlement and a sense of identity that is very deceiving.

That leads right into the third thorn which will grow up and choke the Word of God in our heart and that's *"the desire for other things."*

This is when we desire and pursue things outside of the dominion of God. *'If I could just have this position; if I could just have this marriage; if I could just have this bank balance; if I could just have this education; If I could just drive this car; if I could just have this spiritual gift . . then I know I would be happy.'*

We pray for it because we want it to be God's will for us but that appetite pulls us out of our lane and away from God's best for us. It's the appetite itself which creates the thorns which choke the promises of God over our life.

My sincere prayer for you as I write these words is that you would grow profoundly in this area of trust. I pray that you will come to a place where you can say, *"I only want what comes from God's hand. I will not pursue anything in life that is not in His heart, His plan, His will for me."* It's the desire for other things which chokes the destiny of God over our life. It has to do with appetite. It has to do with stewardship. It has to do with the divided mind. These are the areas that, monitored well, keep us in our lane, so that when our journey on earth finally comes to an end, we will hear those incredible words, *"Well done, good and faithful servant."*

I have certainly been praying that over my own life, that I will see every word God has promised fulfilled; that He will be revealed for Who He truly is through every thought, word and deed in my life. I pray that over you too, I pray that the Lord would help us all to be good stewards of His Word. If we truly want to see God's Kingdom come and God's will done in us, through us and around us, then we really need to get this parable. If we want to live 'on earth as it is in heaven' every moment of every day, then we need to understand what Jesus is teaching here about the priority of the Word of God.

We need to receive the truth which Jesus gave His disciples that day and the truth He is giving us today through His Holy Spirit when He says: *"To you it has been given to know the mystery of the Kingdom of heaven."* So let me encourage you to personalise that again and say these words out loud:

**To me it has been given to know
the mystery of the Kingdom of heaven**

I believe that a lot of the mystery of the Kingdom of heaven has been revealed already thus far in this book. So, I really encourage you to go back and re-visit that teaching and let God open your eyes, your ears and your heart to the wonder, the glory and the life-changing reality of truly living on earth as it is in heaven.

However, I need to warn you that the real meat of this teaching is still to come. Living on earth as it is in heaven is no picnic! Everything in this broken, dysfunctional world is programmed to reject everything we will manifest in the Kingdom of heaven!

I expect the next chapter in particular will contain some rather large chunks of juicy spiritual meat upon which to chew – and large enough to choke some of us if we have not allowed God to prepare us through these first nine chapters.

Therefore, if you have the courage to continue this journey as we explore what really happens when the kingdom of heaven becomes a reality in us and around us, then I look forward to us wrestling with some hard truths in the pages ahead.

CHAPTER TEN
The Hard Truth

Let me establish something right up front: you don't live in a kingdom. I accept that we currently have a Monarch, King Charles III, but you don't live in a kingdom. In fact, even if you moved to England, where the Monarchy is far more important, you still would not be living in a kingdom – in spite of being part of what they call the United Kingdom. They are not united – Scotland can't wait to break away and Ireland may be next and they are certainly not a kingdom in the true sense of the word. In fact, they haven't been a kingdom for over 1,000 years.

England has a King and Australia, as a Commonwealth nation, has the same King but we don't have to think about him at all. In our day-to-day life we never have to refer to the King for any decisions we make. Now I think he is a fine man and I believe a committed Christian, as was his recently departed mother, Queen Elizabeth II. But for all of my life I've pretty much ignored our Monarch and so have you.

Our King today has very little power. There are a few things he can do but they're really quite insignificant. He does them superbly as a figurehead but he is not sovereign over his kingdom. He reigns, but he doesn't rule and there is a difference. The first essential thing to a kingdom is a King who reigns <u>and</u> rules. We don't have that. We have a constitutional Monarchy and that means our Monarch does rule and therefore, He does not tell us what to do.

The requirement to have a true kingdom is to have subjects who obey the sovereign. The two essential components of a true kingdom are a sovereign who rules and subjects who are ruled. Only when you've got those two things, do you have a real kingdom.

It's because we are not a kingdom and have never lived in a true kingdom that we don't really understand the phrase, *the kingdom of God* or *the kingdom of heaven*. We therefore often treat God more like a constitutional Monarch, someone we might wheel out on public occasions but not a God Who truly rules us as His subjects.

If you were in a Jewish home and you sat down for a meal, they would address God before they touch the food, as *'King of the Universe'* and that's the basic Jewish understanding of God. In fact, in many languages in the world, King and God are the same word.

So, God is King of the universe. He is King of nature. He is King of history. I remember a chorus I used to sing as a boy, *'God is still on the Throne'* and it used to give me the feeling of confidence and security. The truth is, God is still on the throne of our universe, whether we acknowledge Him or not, and clearly most people don't.

Now I want to suggest to you that the biggest enemy of our faith is not atheism, but deism. There are people in our churches who really believe that God is what deism believes He is. Deism says God created the universe, but He no longer controls it.

Therefore, you don't pray about such things as the weather. Because God has created nature and nature now runs on its own laws. Almost as if nature is a big clock. God created the clock, but now it's wound up and ticking and there is nothing that we can do about that, or even that God can do about it. Well, I know from personal experience that God can change the weather. He created nature, and He can control it if He so desires!

God also controls history. He is the King of the nations. He is King of kings, the Lord of lords and He is in control over things like elections. He has the casting vote.

That does not mean that everything that happens is God's doing but it does mean that He has the last word and so sometimes He will give us the government we need and at other times He will give us the government we deserve! But God has the casting vote because He is King of the universe.

Humanity is losing the concept of kingdoms. For example, since 1914 at least 24 crowned heads of Europe have just disappeared. That's 24 kingdoms which have completely vanished and those who have kept a royal family have cut them off from ruling and just have a constitutional Monarch as a figurehead position, but a true kingdom does not exist anymore. So less and less of the people in our current world understand the reality of a kingdom.

That's why just mentioning the Kingdom of God or the Kingdom of heaven means very little to most people. By contrast, in Bible times almost every nation was a kingdom and therefore the Bible doesn't ever fully define the kingdom of God. People would have understood what was meant straight away, because they all lived in kingdoms.

However, it's a strange idea, to Britain, to most of Europe and certainly to us in Australia – this idea of having a king who rules a kingdom without a government, without elections, without a parliament, without an opposition, without anything that we take for granted in a democracy. That's because the Bible has no room for democracy. You won't find it anywhere in the Bible.

Now I have probably seen the film *The Ten Commandments* a dozen times and it's a great film, but the now famous director, Cecil B DeMille, made a speech when the film was released and he said this amazing thing, *"This film is about the beginnings of Western democracy."* That's nonsense! This film was based on the Bible and the Bible doesn't ever mention democracy – not once!

The Bible only speaks of a theocracy – where God is King of the universe and we are all His subjects. Why then don't we want a kingdom? Why do we pursue a democracy? Why do we love having elections? Well, it gives us the power so we can kick a government out within a few years of them being voted in. That's democracy - it gives the ordinary people power - and that's one of the most serious challenges to the Kingdom of heaven being released on earth, as we'll see.

Of course, when you look at nature and history, it doesn't look like God is in control. We must face the fact that there are terrible things that happen, like earthquakes, tornadoes, tsunamis, cyclones, bushfires etc. They kill hundreds and thousands of people. In the face of such destruction, it's not easy to believe in a good God Who is in control. When you look at human history and you see the slaughter that has gone on, with humans killing each other, by the thousands, by the millions. It's hard to reconcile.

There has not been a period of ten years in all of history without war, not even ten years of peace! In fact, since 'the war to end all wars' there have been thirty-six more wars! We say that God is the King of history, so why on earth does all this keep happening?

Human beings have always wrestled with the great contrast and the contradiction between what we see and what we believe. There are many ways that we have ingeniously tried to solve this problem. One is called dualism. That is the belief that there are two Gods - one is good and one is bad. Sometimes we will benefit from the good God and sometimes the bad God takes over. That's called dualism. There are others who say, the answer is in polytheism - 'poly' meaning many. With this way of thinking there are many gods and you've got to keep them all happy. The first question then when things go bad is 'which God did we upset or do we have to appease?'

Then there have been real debates about God Himself - and here's the big dilemma. Is God all powerful? Is God good? If He is both of those, then why doesn't He stop all the wars?

Why does He allow evil and suffering to run rampant? Why does He seemingly turn a blind eye to what's happening in our world? Some conclude that God is weak and He can't solve the problems and is just waiting for us to help him.

That's not the answer but even inside Church I am hearing more and more people imply that God is weak. If God is all powerful then you've got to tackle the other question and conclude that God is not good. He's just playing games with us and we are helpless putty in His hands. Therefore, we can't complain – we are just His creatures and we've got to accept His will regardless of whether good things or bad things happen.

Of course, neither of those answers come from the Bible where it states hundreds of times that God is both good and all powerful. We are therefore left with the question, *'Why do things happen as they do?'* Until we face this question squarely and honestly, we won't understand the rest of the Bible at all.

The only explanation is that there must be more than one kingdom operating in the world. Now that is the Bible's answer. There is more than one king and more than one kingdom.

In fact, every member of the human race, wants their own kingdom. The first human beings, said, *'God, we're not going to let you tell us what to do. We will decide for ourselves, what's good and bad for us, and what's right and wrong.'* Adam and Eve made that choice. They wanted their own kingdom over which they could be sovereign. If they wanted that fruit, forbidden or not, they would decide for themselves – and they did.

Every single one of us has now been tainted by that desire to have our own little kingdom. Your home can be your kingdom; your family can be your kingdom; and you can rule like a king or queen. But it's bigger than that – it impacts all areas of life in our society.

We have seen many kingdoms grow in the commercial world. A person starts a small business but then it must grow bigger, because the boss wants a big kingdom - and he will soon have a king's car to drive and soon have branches opening everywhere. There is hardly a human being who has gone into business who hasn't started building up his own kingdom, preferably with his own name everywhere.

In the political world you find the same thing: a politician wants to promote himself as king and build a much larger kingdom, which he can control. Even in the church realm we see someone set up a church and then they want more churches under their name and pretty soon they too are building a kingdom. It happens in almost every sphere we touch, this rebellion against God which says, *'You're not to be king of this. I am king here, or I'm queen here ... and you don't tell me what to do.'*

Now the Bible just calls all that what it is: sin. To establish and grow your own kingdom, be your own boss and declare independence from God is rebellion. It's sin. So, in our world today God is King of the universe, but human beings are kings and queens in their own little kingdoms.

The Bible also tells us that behind all these human kings and man-made kingdoms, there's something else – or someone else actually – and that is the devil, whom the Bible calls 'the king of this world.' When you understand human rebellion and your desire to have your own kingdom and add to that the devil as the king of this broken world, you can now explain everything that is happening around us.

To understand this world and our place in it, we have to accept the Bible's teaching which makes it crystal clear that human beings are not at the top of creation. Evolution has gotten hold of our mindset so that we think mankind is at the top of creation as the most developed creature there is. That makes us rather proud – but it just isn't true. We are not at the top of creation. We are above the animals, but we are below the angels in God's creation.

There is a whole level of life operating above us that has more intelligence, more strength and more speed. Angels can travel around the universe far quicker than our fastest jets. Now, unless you really do believe in angels, you just won't understand the worldview of the Bible. The angels were created superior to human beings and we need to remember that.

Just as human beings have rebelled against their Creator and said, *'We want our own kingdom, where we rule and where our will is sovereign,'* the same thing happened among the angels – long before we ever showed up.

In fact, a third of the angels rebelled against the Kingdom of heaven and this insight is essential to our understanding the Bible's view of our world. Among this third of the angels who rebelled is a lead angel called Lucifer or Satan. The Bible also calls him the devil and He behaves like a dragon who has his own kingdom, and his kingdom is this world. In the Bible he is called 'the god of this world,' also 'the prince of this world' and 'the ruler of this world.' The New Testament also says that we may know that we belong to God, but the whole world lies in the hands of the evil one – this earthly king – Satan.

Now we can begin to understand why the world is in such a mess – it's because we are in complete rebellion against the Kingdom of Heaven.

The rebellion in heaven which Satan led, is still happening right now. Human beings are in rebellion against heaven within their own personal kingdoms and Satan and his fallen angels have set up their kingdom on earth.

Do you know that Satan has even managed to change the Lord's Prayer? Towards the end of that model prayer Jesus gave us is the line, *'deliver us from evil.'* That's what many translations give us and that's what most of us have learned growing up and prayed thousands of times, I'm sure. However, the Greek word translated 'evil' here can also be translated 'evil one' and most of the main translations today now use 'evil one' rather than 'evil.'

Now of course, one of Satan's oldest tricks is to persuade us that he doesn't exist as a person and that evil is just a thing or some impersonal, random force. Satan is a created being and so are all those fallen angels who rule this world.

But Satan doesn't want us to think about him as an actual personal enemy which is why he's very happy for us to pray 'deliver us from evil' rather than to think there are actual beings involved in all that is wrong in our world. That's the first characteristic of the devil's kingdom: deception - which is why Jesus called him 'the father of lies.'

Let me just run through the other characteristics of Satan's kingdom - since his kingdom is this world in which you and I are living today. Deception is the first one and darkness is also a main characteristic of Satan's kingdom. Light is the kingdom of the Lord and we come into His light from the darkness. Satan never opened a day club - it was always a night club - and most of Satan's evil is done in darkness.

In Nazi Germany, the Gestapo came to your house at three o'clock in the morning, when you didn't expect them. That was characteristic of all the Nazi Gestapo activities and all the arrests of the Jews and the enemies of the state.

Satan rules the kingdom of darkness and he loves to hide things. He hates to have his works brought into the light and exposed for everyone to see. Satan conceals – Jesus reveals. Always remember that.

So, Satan's kingdom is a kingdom of deception, a kingdom of darkness. It's also a kingdom of disease. That's one of his biggest weapons in the human realm and that's why you see so much healing take place when Jesus showed up as His kingdom began to overtake the kingdom of darkness.

Now of course the easiest way to conquer any enemy is to divide them and Satan loves to divide Christians from one another or set them against one another. Satan's kingdom is also built on division among human beings.

The final 'D' for us to remember is death. In John 10:10 we read where Jesus said Satan comes to kill, steal and destroy. Now if you've done any work among young people, you will see the death that Satan brings. I'm not just talking about physical death, though it does include that and drugs and suicide are responsible for taking so many young lives. I'm talking about spiritual death – disconnection from God - that's one of Satan's main objectives. He wants people to turn away from the Father. When the prodigal son came home, the father said, *"This is my son who was dead ..."* But he wasn't physically dead - he was living it up in Antioch, spending all his money and having a great time. But all that time he was dead to his Father. And it's that kind of death which is characteristic of Satan's kingdom.

Look at the people today in your own community - go and talk to them about the gospel and you will see what reception you get from most of them. It's amazing how utterly dead people can be towards spiritual things. In many of them there is absolutely no response. Their desire for God and the things of God has completely gone.

That kind of death is horrible. People are alive in the flesh, but dead in their spirit and unless they are born again, and supernaturally regenerated, that's how they will stay.

So that's the Bible's explanation as to why this world is in such a mess and it's been in that mess from almost the very beginning. It is because people have rejected the will of God as their rule of life. It's because so many angels have also rejected God's rule.

When Jesus began His ministry after His baptism, what was the first thing He did? He disappeared into the wilderness to spend time with Satan, before spending time with God's people - an interesting priority. Jesus recognized the real power that was holding people in bondage and unless He first bound 'the strong man', He could not liberate all his victims.

Of course, that doesn't make sense to people who don't believe in Satan or his power in this world and so they do not have the ammunition to handle so many situations in this broken world. They are therefore left to blame God when things go wrong. Hasn't this always been the case? We blame God for the wars that <u>we</u> start, and that <u>we</u> fight. But God didn't start the war and He not responsible for our choices. When you only have a vague idea that God is in total control of everything that happens then you are locked into blaming Him for all the bad things and thereby get sucked into the devil's greatest lie.

All of this raises a huge question and it's the question God is asking us. *'Why do you want Me to be sovereign when you don't want to be subject to My will?'* That has been the problem since the Garden of Eden. We want a sovereign God, but we don't want to be subject to Him – which means we really don't want a sovereign God! If God is sovereign, then He is sovereign according to <u>His</u> will, not ours.

We all want God to do things that <u>we</u> decide He should be doing. I hear it all the time in the church and I read it on the Facebook pages of Christians. We tell God what He needs to do but stop short of accepting His sovereignty over what we do. We make our own choices and then try to tell God what His choices should be.

'Let God be God' is only a quaint catchphrase because for God to really be God in our life, we must subject ourselves to Him completely. That means our whole mind, our will, our emotions, our body, our health, our possessions, our money, our ambition, our work life, our home life, our leisure time; absolutely everything in complete submission to God.

To ask God to heal our bodies, when we are not willing to put our bodies under His control and Lordship, is sheer hypocrisy. We plead with God to bring revival but ignore the call of Jesus to embrace His mission personally and share the gospel with those He leads our way. We treat God like our earthly King. We are happy for Him to reign as our constitutional Monarch and we honour Him to a point and say really nice things about Him; we are even happy to listen to His Easter and Christmas message – but we stop short of allowing Him to rule as our Sovereign – every day.

This is why the Kingdom of heaven is not visible in our world and even in many churches. For the average person living in our nation today and for many attending church meetings each week, they do not see the reality of Kingdom of heaven where Jesus Christ rules and reigns and where His disciples surrender and submit to Him in every area of their lives. If we truly mean what we say when we pray, *"Your Kingdom come, your will be done on earth as it is in heaven,"* then that will require everything we are, everything we own, everything we think, say, and do, to be brought into submission to the King.

CHAPTER ELEVEN
The Presence of the Future

Have you have seen a painting called, *The King of Kings?* It was painted by an artist called Charles E. Butler back in 1916 and first displayed in the Royal Academy in London.

Sadly, the original was destroyed in a bombing raid in the second world war but there are a number of prints and photos circulating. You can view the painting online here:

https://robertgriffith.net/files/the-king-of-kings.jpg

There is some amazing detail in the painting but you really need to look at it very closely because in the picture are portraits of over one hundred and thirty earthly kings and rulers – many of whom have been identified by eagle-eyed historians.

The key figure in the centre is the King of Kings, Jesus Christ. Behind Him, is Satan, the king of this world. Every one of the faces shows the attitude of that king or queen towards the King of Kings. It's quite a unique painting and they have never been able to repeat the luminosity of the robes of the King of Kings. It truly is an amazing picture which portrays life as it really is.

In this chapter I want to explore how God is re-establishing or restoring His kingdom on earth as it is in heaven. God is in the process of putting things right which have been terribly wrong for a very long time because of our sin and rebellion.

This is the most important part of understanding the gospel of the Kingdom. In fact, the whole Bible is about God's remedy and His re-establishment of His Kingdom rule and reign in our world and it all began a very long time ago.

As I am sure you know, when we are introduced to Abraham in the Bible, he is far too old to be of much use by human standards and certainly too old to be a father again. But we soon learn that where mankind finishes - God starts. What is impossible for us, is always possible for God. I am looking forward to meeting this dear old man, because without Abraham, none of us would even be here. You certainly wouldn't be reading this book!

Abraham was a great man and in spite of his advanced age, he left a well-established home and lived in a tent for the rest of his life. Not many 90-year-old men that I know would be willing to do that. I don't think I would. But Abraham consented to live in a tent for the rest of his days when he left all that was familiar and journeyed into the unknown in response to the call of a God nobody knew.

That's when God really began to re-establish His Kingdom on earth and from that man came an entire nation; a nation that began in slavery; a nation that had no time of its own; no money of its own; nothing at all of its own. When you are slaves, you belong entirely to someone else.

So that dear old man's descendants became a nation. God said, *"I'm going to show you my power first and then my authority later."* I want you to get hold of that. God showed the power of His Kingdom first, and then spoke about the lifestyle of His kingdom. That's the order in which we are called to preach the Kingdom of heaven. The gospel of the Kingdom is first demonstrated and then it is declared. It is experienced first and explained next.

Therefore, the power of the Kingdom of heaven must first be displayed on earth, otherwise, why should people accept this Kingdom? Once the power of the Kingdom of heaven is demonstrated, you then declare the Kingdom itself and the authority of the King.

The power first and the authority second - that's how God dealt with Israel. He showed His power first by overcoming Pharaoh, by sending those plagues on Pharaoh's kingdom, to set His people free from slavery. Only then, having gotten them away from Pharaoh; having given them their freedom, did God tell them how He wanted them to live.

Now that order is so important: let the people see first, then let them hear. Demonstrate the Kingdom, then describe it. That's how God Himself deals with people on earth who desire to see His Kingdom re-established here. He even gave Moses anti-magical powers with his staff, so when Pharaoh's magicians tried their best to stop it happening, Moses' magic was better than theirs and this demonstration through the plagues was a very important part in setting the people free from slavery.

This was the first step and then having gotten them to Sinai, God gave them laws, and revealed His will for the way they were to live as His people. We have God's instructions in the book of Exodus, and later, in the book of Deuteronomy. Deuteronomy means 'second law.'

So twice, God gave His instructions as to how they were to live in His Kingdom on earth. So, Israel was called to demonstrate the Kingdom of heaven on earth so that all the other nations could see what living on earth as it is in heaven really looks like.

That was the story of the Old Testament - but I'm afraid it's a sad story. It's a story of how Israel wanted God to be sovereign over all their enemies and over all their troubles but they didn't really want to be His subjects.

As we saw in the previous chapter, the King reigns and rules in a true kingdom. But Israel did not want to be ruled - and so they paid a very high price.

Now before we look at the New Testament, I want to really underline this point. God first delivered His people from slavery with a demonstration of His power - then He gave them His laws. He demonstrated His power first, then His authority as King and that is how Jesus taught the disciples. So, let's come to Jesus, the King of kings and see what He did to re-establish the kingdom of heaven on earth.

Most of Jesus' teaching is about the Kingdom of heaven or the Kingdom of God, those terms are used interchangeably. Over and over again we read, *"The kingdom of God is like this, and like that."* Often, Jesus said it's like a man or a woman.

It's made up of individuals. We also note that the very first preaching of John the Baptist and of Jesus - was identical. *"Repent, for the kingdom of God is at hand."*

Now what does 'at hand' mean? Well, I have a large desk at home and there is a lot of stuff on my desk and around my desk and I know my way around it. Everything is 'at hand.'

That means it is within reach. I can pick up a stapler, a calculator, a pen, a file; I have two computers on my large desk and wheels on my chair so I can slide along and use either one. Everything is 'at hand,' it's near and accessible; I don't have to search for it; it's not hidden or under lock and key. Everything I need is 'at hand.'

John the Baptist and Jesus both said the kingdom of God is *'at hand'* - it's within reach; it is near; it is accessible; it is not beyond our grasp or hidden. Of course, the reason this was so, is because the King had come and wherever the King is, so is His Kingdom.

Now Jesus began His ministry by demonstrating the power of this Kingdom. He healed the sick; He raised the dead; He cast out demons; He read people's thoughts; He controlled the wind and waves; He defied gravity, walking on water.

He constantly demonstrated the power of His Kingdom over and against the kingdom of Satan before He went on to teach the people how to live in the that Kingdom.

The implications here for evangelism are clear: demonstrate the power of the Kingdom of heaven before you preach it and teach it. As we saw earlier in Matthew 10, Jesus told His disciples to go into a town and demonstrate the power of the Kingdom by healing the sick, cleansing the lepers, raising the dead and casting out demons and then to tell the people that the Kingdom of heaven has now come.

This is the same divine order as when God delivered His people from slavery and then taught them how to live under His rule and reign: show them first, tell them second. Jesus did the same.

Now the church has pretty much ignored that order ever since but it's an obvious way to do it. I thank God that there are still Christians today who are praying for healing and demonstrating the power of the Kingdom of heaven first and telling people that the Kingdom of has come.

Then they tell them the rest of the story: *"If you want to embrace the reality of God's kingdom you can do that right now. But it involves a complete re-think of your life, your purpose and where your identity comes from."*

To embrace the fullness of the Kingdom of heaven, we need to step down as the king or queen of our own kingdom and become a subject of the one true King – Jesus Christ.

When you study all of Jesus' teaching on the Kingdom of heaven you will notice there is a present aspect to this Kingdom and a future Kingdom reality. George Eldon Ladd described it perfectly years ago in his first book on the Kingdom of God when he referred to it as *'the presence of the future.'* This means the kingdom is 'now' and 'not yet.'

It has been inaugurated now but it will be consummated in the future. For the discerning, they can enter the Kingdom now; they can see other people in the Kingdom now, but they are also looking forward to the Kingdom being fully established on earth in the future. That will come when the King comes back. It's as simple as that.

At the moment, the King of Kings is invisible – He is present through His Holy Spirit. When the King returns to fully establish His Kingdom, every eye shall see Him and the 'now" of the Kingdom will completely replace the 'not yet.'

Here we must learn something from Israel. Israel had a King from the very beginning - the King of heaven - and He told them how to live. The trouble was, He was invisible to the world and every other nation had a visible King and they could show him off in battle as he rode ahead of his troops.

This lack of a visible king in Israel became a crisis and you can read about it in 1 Samuel 8. Israel wanted a king like other nations - they wanted a visible king. They already had a King – the King of heaven was their King. They were already in His Kingdom or could be. But they said, *"No, we want a visible King."* God finally said, *"All right, I'll give you a king – but this will be your downfall. You will find out what an earthly king is like."*

God gave them Saul, from the tribe of Benjamin. Saul was head and shoulders above everybody else and chosen for his size and strength. They were so glad to finally have a big king who could look down on everybody and intimidate their enemies. That's the kind of king they wanted.

Well, I am sure you know the story ... just as their true King, God, had warned them, things went seriously wrong, very quickly. So much so that God Himself chose someone else to be King.

Even while Saul was still king, God chose a young shepherd boy, David who was the youngest of his family and nothing like the kind of King Israel has envisaged.

However, under King David, the empire of Israel expanded to the limits that God had set for them and even to this day, the Jews look back on the reign of King David as their greatest time in history.

But even the best earthly kings die and I'm afraid that King David also blundered badly before he died. In just one afternoon, he broke all ten commandments. That's quite an achievement! As a result, his kingdom began to decline and his son Solomon was so ambitious for his own wealth, and for his own reputation that under King Solomon, all the seeds were sown for Israel's demise. As soon as he died, civil war broke out and ten tribes broke away from the two in the south called Judah and Benjamin and Israel's story went downhill from there.

So, Israel only had three Kings who ruled over all of the people. The first of those was no good and finished up consulting a medium and the third was no good because of his ambitions for himself and as soon as he died, the nation fractured.

When you read the book of Kings, you'll find most of them were bad kings. In fact, the Northern ten tribes never had a good king. The southern two tribes did have some good ones, but most of them were bad too. When you've got a bad king making all the rules and the people follow, it's no surprise when the nation falls apart - and that's what happened.

But God gave His people a promise, *"I will give you a king like David, a son of David, descended from David, from your royal family, but he will be more than any king before him. He will indeed be king of Israel forever."* (See 2 Samuel 7).

This was the promise of the Messiah, and that word means 'anointed king.' In Greek, the word *Messiah* becomes the word *Christ*, which is from the word *Chrism*.

You may be interested to know that when Queen Elizabeth was crowned on 2nd June 1953 in Westminster Abbey, she was anointed with oil which was called the Chrism and she herself said that this was the most moving moment in the whole ceremony for her.

So, when you call Jesus 'Christ' that's not His surname. When you say *Jesus Christ* you are actually saying, '*Jesus, my anointed King.*'

Some days I wish we would actually use the word King instead of Christ, because that's what we really mean. Jesus is God's anointed King. He has the *Chrism* of the Holy Spirit - the anointing oil of the Holy Spirit, which He has to a greater degree than any other king who ever existed.

So that's how the Kingdom of heaven came to earth, in Jesus, and that's how it's going to be re-established on earth. This Kingdom of Christ is expanding today faster than it has ever expanded in more than 2,000 years. Every minute I sit here typing words, there are more than fifty new voices proclaiming Jesus as Christ somewhere in the world.

Sadly, that is not the case in most western nations – but in Africa, South America and even among Muslims in the Middle east, thousands of people every day are coming to Jesus, the Christ as the church continues to grow.

But the church is not the Kingdom of heaven, it's a colony of the kingdom if you like. It is wrong to think that building the church is building the kingdom. When that mistake is made you end up with pastors and elders who begin to think they are little kings and queens and they start ruling. We really don't want that.

But every time a person is brought to Christ and filled with the Holy Spirit, the Kingdom of heaven is expanding and what began as a tiny seed, like the mustard seed, becomes a great tree, in which the birds of heaven can nest and this is happening today on a larger scale than ever before.

Jesus said, *"I will build my Church"* and that is what He is doing today. However, that is not visible to the world in most places because we are not demonstrating the power of the Kingdom in the church.

The power of the Kingdom of heaven is made visible when the reality of that Kingdom unfolds within this kingdom just like we see in the book of Acts when the Church began on earth: people being healed, delivered, saved and transformed by the power of God – that's the Kingdom of heaven in action!

When people today get to see what the people saw in the book of Acts, they will be drawn to this phenomenon and they will listen to the gospel of the Kingdom. But not until they *see* something will they be willing to *hear* anything.

Now let's go back to the fact that Jesus talked about the Kingdom of heaven on the one hand as a present, steady growth but also there are those parables that talk about a future reality. For example, as we saw earlier, one parable talks about the Kingdom of heaven being like a man sowing seed in his field.

That parable speaks about the growth of the Kingdom of heaven through the Word of God right now – before our very eyes, just like seed sown in good soil. We can see it germinate and grow and bear fruit and the Kingdom of heaven is growing every day and we need to really believe this for our encouragement because we may not see that around us in our part of the world yet, but the Kingdom of heaven is growing on earth.

Then there is the future aspect of the Kingdom. One day the King will return and then He will establish His Kingdom fully. Every Christian believes Jesus is coming back, but hardly anyone ever asks why. Why is the King coming back? What is He coming back to do? How long will He stay this next time? The answer is He's going to stay a very long time next time, and long enough to rule our world. Then, and only then, will the words of Revelation 11:15 be true, *"The nations of the world have become the kingdom of our God and His Christ."*

That's the end game! That's what we are ultimately praying for when we cry out to God, *"Your kingdom come, Your will be done on earth, as it is in heaven."* We are praying for the Kingdom of heaven to be consummated and established in this world visibly. We are praying for the day to come when the King of King sits on His throne and is finally embraced as the King of the whole universe.

Then, and only then, will that incredible painting by Charles E. Butler from over a hundred years ago become a reality when the king of this world, Satan, loses his throne and all the earthly kings, queens and rulers fall on their knees before the King of Kings and the Lord of Lords.

On that glorious day, all the great stories of the Bible will merge into one reality and find their fullest meaning in the powerful reality of the Kingdom of Heaven on earth.

Moses, Abraham, Noah, David, Ruth, Jeremiah, Mary, Joseph, Jesus, Peter, Paul, every journey and every story of God's people over the centuries will finally make sense when the Christ, the Messiah, the King of Heaven, reigns and rules over all His Kingdom.

That glorious day is when every knee will bow and every tongue confess that Jesus Christ is the Lord of all creation. What a glorious day that will be!

CHAPTER TWELVE
The Core Value of the Kingdom

At this point in our study, I think we need to wrestle with a very obvious but vitally important question: *How do we know when the Kingdom of Heaven has come to earth?* In some ways I have already answered that in previous chapters. We will know the Kingdom has come when we see and experience the reality of heaven in this earthly kingdom.

The sick will be healed; the spiritually dead will be raised; the oppressed will be set free; the lost will be found; the blind will see; the deaf will hear; the lame will dance and the list goes on. That is evidence of the Kingdom of heaven.

However, we need to go deeper than that. We need to know why those things are manifesting around us. We need to understand what lies at the very centre of the Kingdom of heaven coming to earth.

Recently I was reading the account of the crucifixion of Jesus again. I've read it thousands of times and preached on it hundreds of times, but on this occasion, something hit me really hard – like never before in my long journey with God.

Jesus has just been betrayed, arrested, falsely accused and tried, found guilty and sentenced to death. On the way to His death, He is beaten, abused, mocked and spat upon. After being nailed to the cross, the mocking continues as He experiences humanity at its worst and feels the agony and pain of the whole world's sin come crushing down upon His broken, dying body.

In the midst of that brutal reality, Jesus says something which is incomprehensible to us. He says, *"Father, forgive them, for they don't know what they are doing."*

Now most of us in the church understand forgiveness. We have to understand forgiveness if we are going to walk with the Lord. However, I want to point out that it is possible to embrace the philosophy of forgiveness, without the practice of forgiveness. In other words, we can hold to the value of forgiveness, but not necessarily embrace the daily practice of forgiveness. We may know the theory, but we can still struggle in the practical area.

Now we've all had bad experiences where someone has betrayed us or turned on us in some way and wounded us. Our emotions kick in then and we feel hurt, disappointed, even angry. Usually, we need some time then to cool down, take a breath, get over the shock and pain, before we can even think about forgiveness. This may take days, months or even years before we can genuinely forgive that person.

That's why these words of Jesus are so incomprehensible! Here He is in the middle of the most horrible thing that's ever happened to any human being; He is experiencing the worst physical, emotional and spiritual pain a human being could ever endure; He is looking directly into the eyes of His murderers, His mockers, and as that crescendo of brutality towards Him reaches its peak, Jesus asks His Father to forgive these people!

Just think about this, *"they don't know what they are doing?"* They knew they were crucifying an innocent man! They knew that they had just released a guilty criminal in His place! They knew from His reputation, His ministry, His works, just how he had served in that city and that region for three and a half years.

They knew His reputation; they knew about His miracles; the multiplying of food; the many healings and deliverance, the number of people celebrating His teaching as it brought such life to so many - they knew all of that.

But yet from the perspective of Jesus, they didn't know what they were really doing, and so He cried out to God for their forgiveness! Here's the fulfilment of a prophetic word back in Isaiah, that this One who would bear the sin of many would be interceding for those who are the most guilty.

> *"... because he poured out his life unto death, and was numbered with the transgressors. For he bore the sin of many, and made intercession for the transgressors."* (Isaiah 53:12)

Now this is fascinating to me because, first of all, we know that Jesus is entirely God, and entirely man, that's almost impossible for us to fully comprehend. As someone once described it: *He was God as though He were not man at all and He was a man as though He were not God at all.*

So here we have Jesus, the man, praying for the forgiveness of His enemies. We know this is Jesus the man praying, because Jesus as God would just pronounce forgiveness, He wouldn't have to pray to His Father. So, Jesus the man is praying and asking His Father in heaven to forgive the ones who can't possibly deserve forgiveness! The mind boggles.

Why was it important for Jesus to pray that kind of a prayer? The answer is simple. Forgiveness has to be measurable in action. It can't be a philosophy. It can't just be a deeply held belief, it has to be measurable. So, what did Jesus do? He interceded on behalf of the most guilty people on the planet! That is forgiveness!

If somebody has stolen money from you, forgiving them doesn't mean you give them the password to your bank account so they can take the rest. You don't condone or encourage them in their sin. Forgiveness means you take care of your own heart, so that even your thought life is evidence of your genuine forgiveness. True forgiveness is measurable through our practice.

So, Jesus hanging on a cross, prays out loud for all to hear and record and for us to read and understand throughout all history; He prays that God the Father will forgive the people who are about to murder His only Son!

Ok, so now let me answer the question I posed at the beginning of this chapter by sharing some of the most beautiful, but most confronting words in the Bible.

> *Love is patient, love is kind. It does not envy, it does not boast, it is not proud. It does not dishonour others, it is not self-seeking, it is not easily angered, it keeps no record of wrongs. Love does not delight in evil but rejoices with the truth. It always protects, always trusts, always hopes, always perseveres. Love never fails." (1 Corinthians 13:4-8)*

The core value of the Kingdom of Heaven is love and the most powerful manifestation of love is forgiveness.

God created us in love, for love. God forgave us, redeemed us, transformed us and welcomed us into His Kingdom because of love. Jesus became one of us because the love of God was greater than the sin of mankind. Jesus was nailed to that cross because of love and forgiveness flowed freely from His love.

We see love in action every day in life and ministry of Jesus on earth. Everything He said, everything He did and also refused to do, was all birthed in love. But nowhere was this core value of the Kingdom of heaven more evident and more poignant than on the cross as the life was literally draining out of this man.

Isaiah prophesied that Jesus would be 'numbered among the transgressors' and here is Jesus hanging between two criminals, receiving the same fate as those who deserve death. One of them mocks him and other just asks Jesus to remember him when He comes into His Kingdom.

This man had done nothing to deserve the love of Jesus. He had done nothing to count himself worthy to be called a follower or a disciple. But Love hung on the cross next to him and Love said, *"Today, you will be with me in paradise."*

Here is the Son of God, Who is being crucified because of this man's sins. If there was nobody else on the planet except this one sinner, Jesus would still be crucified for him, and in that moment, Love washes away his sin.

Jesus forgives a criminal next to him and then prays for forgiveness for the guys at his feet who are busy gambling for His clothing; and for the religious leaders who had been shouting 'crucify!' The most innocent person is forgiving the most guilty and they cast Him aside and watch Him die!

This amazing story is told because His Kingdom has, at its core, the beauty, wonder and the privilege of forgiveness, which flows from the deep wellspring of incomprehensible, unconditional love, which is the essence of our God.

My prayer, and I hope your prayer also, is that by God's grace we will release the Kingdom of heaven on earth every day in some measurable way. Without doubt, at the core of God's Kingdom is love and forgiveness and that flows to us directly from God, Who is love.

> *"This is love: not that we loved God, but that he loved us and sent his Son as an atoning sacrifice for our sins." (1 John 4:10)*

> *"Whoever lives in love lives in God, and God in them. This is how love is made complete among us ... In this world we are like Jesus ... We love because he first loved us."*
> *(1 John 4:17-19)*

May we therefore pray every single day that God will help us demonstrate forgiveness. As God answers that prayer, we might then begin to truly live on earth as it is in heaven!

CHAPTER THIRTEEN
Hidden Treasure

Each week in our local communities we come together as the church; as the people of God; gathered around the Word of God; in the Presence of God. Millions of brothers and sisters join us before the throne of God in worship. But why do we do that? Who are we really? What are we? Why are we even here?

The church is full of all kinds of different people: the broken, the lonely, the wonderers, the wanderers, the hopeful, the enthusiastic, the lost, the passionate and the faithful. For many of them, gathering together each week represents the whole of their church experience. They listen attentively to a sermon, sing a few songs, they are invited to pray and then they'll return to their lives.

But for some, questions will start bubbling to the surface of their faith. Is this the full extent of what Jesus intended for His followers? Who is the church for really? Is this as good as it gets?

I answered those questions in my book, *Being the Church* and you may already know the answers but let me remind you here. The church is not the building where people attend weekly services. It's not a program or an event or a list of rules or a philosophy. The church isn't a political affiliation, a club or a holiday tradition in December. The church is all the followers of Jesus Christ, everywhere.

The Greek word for church, the word behind the concept of church is *ekklesia* and it is the combination of two words *ek*, which means *out* and *kalleo* which means *called*. So, the Church is the *'called out ones'* - the collective body of all the followers of Jesus Christ everywhere who are called out by Jesus for a purpose.

In the beginning of the book of Acts we see where Jesus is calling His disciples to a task, which is to bring something called the gospel, the good news to all the world - and this gospel would go out to all the outsiders: the forgotten, the abandoned; the excluded; and they, those outsiders, would see and receive that gospel as something profoundly good.

However, when Jesus talked about the gospel, it was always in conjunction with something else, something called the Kingdom of God or the Kingdom of heaven, and in the Kingdom of heaven, God's purposes are revealed. There's justice and righteousness, there's hope for the poor and for the oppressed, and in the Kingdom of heaven, mercy and forgiveness triumph over bitterness and resentment.

People previously deemed to be far from God are now brought into His family, adopted as His sons and daughters. The fullness of the Kingdom of heaven, according to Jesus, is not merely expressed as a way for people to secure a ticket to heaven for when they die. Rather, the good news is that God's eternal Kingdom is invading time and space right here now and moving into this present world.

The people who belong to Jesus join Him in His worldwide restoration project – His mission: the re-establishment of His kingdom rule and reign on earth, as it is in heaven.

So, the 'called out ones,' the church, are committed to advancing this good news of God's Kingdom into the world, not as a means of helping people avoid the world but rather to see Kingdom life become real here and now, across the whole church, with the power of the whole gospel, for the blessing of the whole world.

That is who you are. That is why you are here. Any other reason why you are here must come second to God's reason for you being here. Let's take a deep breath and be prepared for what God has for us right now.

I want us to look at just three verses in Matthew chapter 13 and in those three verses we find two parables from Jesus about the Kingdom of Heaven.

> *"The kingdom of heaven is like a treasure hidden in a field. When a man found it, he hid it again, and then in his joy went and sold all he had and bought that field. Again, the kingdom of heaven is like a merchant looking for fine pearls. When he found one of great value, he went away and sold everything he had and bought it." (Matthew 13:44-46)*

The Kingdom of heaven is like a treasure. Do you really feel the weight of those words? The Kingdom of heaven is like a treasure - as opposed to absolutely everything else in our world being fodder and hay and wood and stubble that will burn up in the fire!

But the Kingdom of heaven is like a treasure hidden in a field - a treasure so valuable that this man gave up everything he owned so that he could buy that field and make that treasure his own. It became the most important thing in his whole life. Everything else meant now nothing to him, in comparison to that treasure.

Sadly, we all live in a world where we have many treasures. We are blessed beyond measure and richer than 80% of the people in the world. Which makes it harder for us to grasp this concept of treasuring one thing above everything else. We have many, many 'pearls' in our possession and I am not sure we would easily give them all up for just one 'pearl' of great value.

We live in a culture which teaches us to believe that more is better and so for many of us, quantity has become more important than quality. Many people will live their whole lives in that mindset. Some lucky ones might have their eyes opened to what a true treasure is and that awakening often comes through a crisis.

I can remember one weekend over forty years ago like it was yesterday. We all have those memories which are burned into our historical timeline and carry more significance than millions of other memories which fade over time.

It was the weekend of 16th-17th April 1983. My wife and I had recently bought our very first home in Orange, NSW. We had also welcomed our first child into the world just eleven months earlier. I had a good job. We loved our new home. We had a good church. Everything was close to perfect and, being a handyman, I was really enjoying all the little projects around the house. On this weekend, I was tackling my largest project to date – a new veranda along the back of our house. I had not built one before so I enlisted the help of my dad. We spent two long days together and produced a pretty awesome result and I ended up spending more time with my father that weekend than I probably had in ten years.

It was a great weekend, but I doubt that it would have remained so clear in my mind so many years later had it not been for another event that unfolded that same week. At 7am the following Thursday our phone rang and it was my sister telling me that dad had suffered a cardiac arrest in his sleep and when mum woke that morning, he was dead. My father was only 54 and my baby sister was only 9.

I learned something in that moment, and even more so in the days that followed. It doesn't matter how rich you are, it doesn't matter how fit you are; it doesn't matter how loved you are; it doesn't matter how blessed you are - you're going to die. It doesn't matter how strong you are, you're going to be weak. Your youth will be gone in the blink of an eye; your will power will disappear in a moment as you vanish and become just a memory. In that moment, everything you lived for doesn't matter anymore, unless it is found within the perfect will of God.

The shock of learning of my father's sudden death was only surpassed by the realisation that I was not prepared for it. I was not prepared for my perfect world to be challenged, much less turned on its head completely.

It was as though God was saying to me, *"Didn't you realise your father was dying? You are dying. Your children are dying, and the world they live in is already dead. This is not supposed to be your home. It should not be your main source of joy and purpose. It's not supposed to be the thing you're focussed on. Why look at a rotting carcass - when there's a treasure before you of infinite value?"*

Now you might think that's a pretty hard word from God at such a time, but very often it is only at such times that we are open to hearing the hard truth from God. He has been saying the same thing to us all throughout history, but we rarely listen.

Throughout all of Scripture, we hear God saying, *"Seek Me ... seek Me ... seek Me ... seek Me and you will find Me ... and I will show you great and mighty things that you do not know and have not heard and have not seen ... seek Me and My kingdom above everything else."*

That's what this parable is all about. When the man found that treasure, at that moment everything else in his life became meaningless. Everything else took second place to that treasure. His greatest passion was directed towards one thing and one thing only. I'm sure he probably had many loves in his life; he probably had many trinkets he called treasures; he probably bothered himself with all sorts of vain activities. But the moment His eyes were focussed on that treasure, absolutely everything else vanished and the only thing he could think about, the only thing he could focus on was what his eyes had seen. From that point forward, that is where his primary passion was directed.

Where is your primary passion directed today? If you were to be brutally honest with yourself right now, would you not admit that the focus of your life, the thoughts of your day and night are more given towards the temporal; more focussed on the things of this world?

Now you might say, *"Well you know, we live in the world, we've got to make money, we've got to eat."* Listen, most people in the world aren't working so hard and striving so much just to eat. It's all the other stuff we crowd into our lives and give value to which costs us so much.

May we hear the voice of the Spirit now. Don't you see, you only have a moment's time on this earth, only a moment. And God is your Father, and your Master and your Keeper and your Provider and He calls you to trust Him and turn away from all the things that glitter but are not gold, and turn to the only thing that matters, Jesus Christ and the coming of His Kingdom.

So, you raise your family as a godly heritage to the Lord and do everything within your means to support the mission of Christ at home and then across the earth.

There are only two aspects of mission - you're either called to go down into the well, or you're called to hold the rope for those who go down.

Either way, there's going to be scars on your hands. It's just as costly to hold the rope as it is to go down and it causes just as many scars.

So where are your scars friend? What has the mission of Christ cost you? What has the Great Commission cost you? What has preparing the Bride of Christ cost you? What has the will of God cost you? Where are your scars? If the Kingdom of heaven is your treasure; if God's Kingdom is your pearl of great price, then you will have scars!

You will gladly pay whatever price you need to pay for that which is more important than anything else in this world. That's what the Apostle Paul means when he exhorts us again right now, through the Holy Spirit:

> *"Since, then, you have been raised with Christ, set your hearts on things above, where Christ is, seated at the right hand of God. Set your minds on things above, not on earthly things. For you died, and your life is now hidden with Christ in God. When Christ, who is your life, appears, then you also will appear with him in glory. Put to death, therefore, whatever belongs to your earthly nature ..."*
> *(Colossians 3:1-5)*

When that man finds this treasure in the field the verse says, *"In his joy ..."* he sold everything to buy the field and secure that treasure. For joy, not for discipline, not for dedication, not for salvation, but in his joy, he sells all that he has and buys that field. Joyfully, willingly, he says, *"Lord, take it. It's yours. Take it all. Nothing compares to this treasure."*

Do you realize what privilege you have? If you're a believer in Jesus Christ, you are the most privileged person on the face of the earth. You have been called to know Him and to be His disciple. There is no greater privilege!

Here is another wonderful but confronting truth. God doesn't need anybody to fulfill His plan and purpose. If all the preachers and all the missionaries on the face of the earth perished today, God would still do what God planned to do. God doesn't *need* anybody.

But God has chosen to open the door and invite us into the holy of holies. He has granted us the privilege of being part of what He is doing. He can do it alone but He doesn't want to. He wants to partner with us, His children, to save the world and advance His Kingdom on earth. Just think about that for a few moments.

Let me sharpen the point some more. The only reason you are alive is because air is free. Your life has no meaning; your clothes have no meaning; your job has no meaning; your money has no meaning; your time has no meaning; your thoughts have no meaning ... other than within the context of God's Kingdom and God's will.

When you truly set your mind and heart on things above and not on earthly things; when you truly seek first the kingdom of God and His righteousness, then at that point, absolutely everything in your life can be filled with true meaning and purpose when it comes under the Lordship of Jesus Christ and when it is all harnessed and directed into fulfilling Christ's mission on earth.

When Jesus rose from the dead, He filled the grave with light and life. Your life is a grave; you were born into this fallen world spiritually dead and nothing about your life impacted the reality of the Kingdom of Heaven.

But when you were raised to life in Christ; when you were born again into the Kingdom of Heaven, everything about your life meant something as it was fully surrendered to God.

Now, your whole life is lived between two days; you live between the day when Christ hung on that cross and the day when all mankind will stand before that same Christ. Those two days are the bookends to your life if you like. They define your life as seen by God within His kingdom.

You are who you are because of the cross of Christ. You live and move and have your being here and now in Christ, for Christ and through Christ and the only reason you and this whole planet are still here is so that you might embrace the mission of Christ to bring all of God's lost children home. Everything else must find its meaning and its significance in that reality or you have missed the whole point of life.

This is not a time for thinking about the world. This is a time for cutting the ropes and letting the wind fill your sails so you can be carried by God fully into His glorious Kingdom purposes.

The most privileged people in the world have the greatest responsibility. God is offering you the greatest privilege to participate with Him in the greatest work any man, woman or young person could imagine.

So those three words are perhaps the greatest prayer we could ever pray, *"Your kingdom come."* However, as I hope you have discerned from this book, if you really want to sincerely pray, *"Your kingdom come,"* then you will need to utter three more words and they will be much harder to say, but without them, God's Kingdom will continue to elude you. Those words are simply *"I surrender all."* You really can't have one without the other.

We will not see the reality and the power and the glory of the Kingdom of heaven while we maintain our own little kingdom. The Kingdom of heaven is that pearl of great price and unless you embrace that pearl as the most valuable thing in your whole live, you will not see God's will done on earth as it is in heaven.

The Kingdom of heaven is that treasure of inestimable value and we will only see the fullness of God's Kingdom come when we surrender control of everything in our own little kingdom and the kingdom of this world. Only then will we personally know the power and reality of Paul's powerful words to the Church all those years ago:

> *"I have been crucified with Christ and I no longer live, but Christ lives in me. The life I now live in the body, I live by faith in the Son of God, who loved me and gave himself for me." (Galatians 2:20)*

www.ingramcontent.com/pod-product-compliance
Lightning Source LLC
Chambersburg PA
CBHW051445290426
44109CB00016B/1675